WOMEN AND WORK

Ross Davies

WOMEN AND WORK

ARROW BOOKS

ARROW BOOKS LTD
3 Fitzroy Square, London W1

An imprint of the Hutchinson Publishing Group

London Melbourne Sydney Auckland
Wellington Johannesburg Cape Town
and agencies throughout the world

First published 1975
© 1975 by Ross Davies

Made and printed in Great Britain
by The Anchor Press Ltd
Tiptree, Essex

ISBN 0 09 910710 4

For Sara and for Charlie

and

In memory of Griffith Eifion Ellis Jones
1932–1973

Contents

Preface

In this book I set out to explore the question: how is it that women, much more than men, have come to do work ill-matched to their individual needs and capacities? It soon became clear that bogeymen were thin on the ground. The villains of the piece, if any, were neither men nor women so much as two linked assumptions common to sexes. One is the widespread belief that the present inequality is a dispensation of Providence, rooted firmly in the wisdom of the ages. The other is that in working at all a woman is somehow untrue to the higher functions of wife and mother. The contrast between the strength of these assumptions and the flimsiness of their justification is a recurring theme in this book.

In drawing attention to what I take to be the neglect of all our interests by the disregard shown to those of women, I risk something that in the book I condemn in others. This is to fall into the habit of generalizing about women as if they were not so much a collection of individuals as a cohesive group with identical qualities and responses. Writers do not, after all, turn out books about men and work. They write about particular kinds of male worker, whether tinker, tailor soldier, priest. However, it seemed a risk worth taking. Men tend to have more interesting jobs than women. It has always been a temptation, therefore, to leave women out of the literature of work, just as for a long time novelists and playwrights thought only the lives of the rich suitable material for the literature of leisure.

It is in fact inherited assumptions about women and work

that I am writing about rather than 'women' as such, although in practice it is impossible to keep the two apart. Women's situation is different, after all. For much of their lives many if not most women have a dual responsibility – that of work and of running a home and family – in a society primarily fashioned by, and for the convenience of, men. As a man, this danger was in my mind from the start. Another point was made to me as I went along.

This was that in singling out work I was merely chipping away at one little corner of a vast edifice of discrimination that took in the loftier themes of relationships between the sexes, the future of the nuclear family and heaven knows what else. There is no shortage of books upon these themes. There are also more and more women, particularly married women, going out to work and, apart from academic studies, little is being written for and about them. The last thing I have tried to do is to write yet another book about women's 'rights'. In this country anybody can still have his or her 'rights' if they choose to push hard enough. Women are the majority sex and they have had the vote for over half a century. In a time when we have to make the most of our resources I have merely tried to highlight an area of confusion and of waste.

Finally, I would like to thank some people for their help. To the late Moira Keenan, a colleague on *The Times*, I must acknowledge a debt, since it was she who first set me thinking along these lines. Eve Macpherson kindly published some preliminary articles of mine. I am indebted to Diana Saville for encouragement and to Philippa Harrison and James Hughes for some sound advice. Any errors are mine. There are throughout the book references to the work of Baroness Seear and of Ivy Pinchbeck. These are insufficient acknowledgement of the admiration I feel for them, and of the help their work has been to me. Mildred Surry of the Fawcett Library, Marian Pearson, formerly of *The Times* Intelligence Department, and Horace Bromley, librarian of *The Times*

Business News kindly steered essential books and official publications my way. Thanks also to Brenda Griffiths and to Julie Harrison, who typed my manuscript.

London, 11 December 1974

1. Working women today: a wasted resource

We in this country have to live on our wits, and half the wits are in the female heads, though one would never think so, looking at the way women are distributed throughout the labour market.

Baroness Seear

Man for the field and woman for the hearth:
Man for the sword and for the needle she:
Man with the head and woman with the heart:
Man to command and woman to obey;
All else confusion.

Tennyson, The Princess

We in these islands live on our wits. That is to say, the natural resource upon which we most depend for our economic wellbeing is the intelligence, ingenuity and adaptability of the people who work. More precisely, we do not live upon all our wits, but on somewhere between a half and two-thirds of them. Those wits which are to be found in female heads are largely ignored by industry, commerce and the professions. Women make up over half the population and a fast-growing third of the labour force. They are, however, excluded from, or conditioned to think themselves unsuitable for, positions of skill or authority. For too long jobs have been classified either as 'men's' or 'women's' work rather than as that of the individual best fitted for the purpose regardless of sex.

In a man's world, women have been the losers in this division of labour. A higher proportion of women's jobs are unskilled, menial, repetitive or poorly-paid than are men's. Yet women are intrinsically no less and no more intelligent, ingenious or adaptable than men. It follows that more women than men are denied the opportunity to use their individual gifts to best advantage in their work. The benefits of those abilities are therefore lost not only to the women concerned but to their employments, and hence to the economic wellbeing of the country in which they live and work. It is a waste, and one that more and more women are beginning to sense. A growing number of women, for reasons we shall examine, are now going to work. Yet they are being largely confined to traditional women's work. They are denied promotion, training and responsibility in a way that ignores their long-established and increasing importance as workers. The justification for this often boils down not to being an unfit individual but simply to being a woman and not a man.

The time has long gone by when we in these islands could support even our most basic needs in food, fuel and metals by what could be mined, fished or grown within or around our own shores. Since, somewhere towards the end of the eighteenth century, we became an industrial rather than an agricultural nation, our population and our expectation of material comfort has increased to the extent that we must look overseas to supplement what we can ourselves produce. To buy the food we eat we must export the products of the efficient use of our wits. These products might be aeroplanes, they might be buttons. But they share a common factor besides the ingenuity that has been invested in them. The very materials from which these exports are made may also have come from abroad, and have therefore had to be bought and paid for from the produce of the country's wits. The abilities of our work-force are therefore a resource to be protected, encouraged and, above all, to be used to the full.

The past century and a half is sometimes presented as a record of continuous social advance. In that time, after all, we have seen the state enact many laws to improve working conditions, and to provide primary and secondary education for all. Today, the proportion of the population graduating is the same as that matriculating in 1945. Moreover, a government that allows many of its citizens to moulder in unemployment, as happened between the two world wars, will now no longer be tolerated.

Today, for the first time since the nation turned from agriculture to industry, we are beginning to see work as a function of people, rather than people as a function of work. We try, with varying success, to create work where there is none, to sustain it where it falters, and to take it to the people rather than the other way about. It might be assumed, therefore, that we make the best use possible out of the 25 million people in paid employment in these islands. This may be so, but there is one glaring exception: the 9 million women members of that work-force.

The number of men in the work-force has hardly altered in twenty years, whereas the proportion of women has increased by a fifth: now they represent over a third, and soon they will be a half. Over half those women are married, and soon the proportion will be nearer two-thirds. By any token, the abilities of these women are a considerable and growing part of the nation's resources. Yet even now, after nearly two centuries of industrialization, it is a potential frittered away for the most part on work that affects not so much the capabilities of the individual women involved as the view which society, women included, holds of what is right or proper for 'women' as a whole.

To make matters worse, the whole situation has for years been wrapped in a self-perpetuating complacency which ensures that this waste is cheerfully countenanced because it is so easy to ignore.

'In Britain', says a Central Office of Information handbook[1] widely circulated for reference material, 'the full participation of women in industry, in the professions and in all kinds of public administration, is today accepted as a normal feature of the national way of life.'

By any standard, this is a remarkable assertion. A very different situation is suggested by the National Federation of Business and Professional Women's Clubs, 1972:

There is normally no shortage of jobs for women. They are welcome as members of the labour force just as long as they are content with unskilled poorly paid work and do not expect the normal opportunity for promotion which a man in a similar position would expect.[2]

These are not the words of a revolutionary but of an organization of doctors, managers and lawyers. When it was written, women represented a third of the work-force but were taking home a fifth of the national pay packet. The fact that such a club could exist is proof that women can rise to positions of responsibility. The writer's point, however, is that their numbers are so few, and their successes have been gained at such cost. Similar points were made by Professor Pigou[3] of Cambridge University, who wrote:

. . . certain occupations are practically shut to women by convention. This fact, by lowering the demand for women's labour, causes the general level of women's wages to be slightly lower than it would otherwise be; and it also damages production by interfering with the most economic use of labour power.

The difference between the two statements is that the first was written in 1972, the second in 1919. In that year, the Sex Disqualification (Removal) Act removed legal bars to the entry into professions of women. But the law had no teeth, and as a result it was never really put to the test. What, then, is the position today, half a century and more later? Of architects only 4 per cent are women. Only 8 per cent of barristers are women, and 1 per cent of chartered accountants. Of engineers, chemical or electrical, only 0·07 per cent are women. Two per cent of solicitors are women, only a fifth of medical practitioners are women. In 1968, of the jobs ranked as managerial in manufacturing industry, 400 000 were done by men, and under 3000 by women. Where, then, are women employed in any great numbers? Between 1951 and 1971, the working population had risen by $1\frac{1}{2}$ million to nearly 25 million, of which all but 69 000 were accounted for by an increase in the number of women coming into the work-force, particularly married women.

There are about 9 million women workers, or about half the female population. Of these, only a third work in manufacturing industry, and the rest are in the service sector. Over a half are in jobs which are ranked as unskilled or semi-skilled, i.e., needing between one and six months' training. In manufacturing industry, the greatest concentration of women is in three areas: food, drink and tobacco; engineering, especially electrical engineering; and textiles, clothing and footwear. The other two-thirds, in the service sector, are also to be found in three main areas: distribution (shops); professional and scientific (nursing, teaching); and miscellaneous services (catering and laundries). Here women outnumber men by three to two. Among manual workers, only one woman in eight, as opposed to nearly one man in three, works in the seven industries where men's average earnings are highest (vehicles, paper, printing and publishing, coal and petroleum), shipbuilding and marine engineering, bricks, pottery and glass, metal manufacture and transport and communications). Yet more than a half of all women employed, compared with a quarter of men, are in the lowest-paying industries: textiles, clothing and footwear, distributive trades, professional and scientific services, public administration, miscellaneous services, agriculture, forestry and fishing.

'Despite their vastly increased numbers, women have continued to work in a range of jobs which have largely been their traditional preserve', says the Office of Manpower Economics.[4] Where men and women work together, the work the women do is likely to be classed as less skilled. In production jobs, half the men are classed as skilled, but less that a quarter of the women. In the professions women outnumber men only in the lowest-paid occupations, teaching and nursing. Few women manual workers are to be found in high-pay industries. Where men work in industries employing many women, the men find their own wages are also low.

The disproportion between the increasing number of women in the work-force and the range of jobs and of responsibility open to them is matched by a persistent inequality in earnings. Women who are full-time manual employees, for example, work fewer hours than men, even where their standard hours are the same. This is partly because legislation and the competing claims of their domestic responsibilities cause women to do less overtime and shiftworking. Even so, however, women's weekly earnings expressed as a percentage of men's fell from 55 to 51 per cent between 1950 and 1970. If we look at average hourly earnings, which are less affected by differences in overtime and shiftworking, then the percentage in 1971 was still only 60 per cent, the same as in 1955 and 1 per cent less than in 1950. At the end of 1975 an Equal Pay Act is to come into force, eighty-seven years after equal pay became Trades Union Congress policy.

This Act seeks to establish the right of women to equal treatment in pay and other conditions of work where they are employed in work that is the same or broadly the same as that done by men or, where different, where the job has been given an equal value under a job evaluation scheme. Unfortunately, of the 9 million working women, only about a half do the same jobs as men. As regards the other half, it is unfortunately quite simple, and quite legal, to circumvent the Act by rigging the job evaluation scheme. There are about 2·5 million women working as typists, office machine operators and sewing machinists, in jobs which are virtually 'women only'. There are nearly 2 million more, working as shop assistants and catering staff, where only one in four employees is a man. Even where men and women work together in named occupations, women tend to be employed at lower levels of skill. Thus, while women outnumber men in clerical work, only 10 per cent of women, compared with 25 per cent of men, are graded as senior clerks. But the Act is not only hardly any guarantee of more equitable treatment for women, it could also prove positively harmful. If the price of women's labour rises faster than their range of job opportunities widens, the Act will increase the pressure on employers to replace that labour with machines.

Women are more likely than men to be unskilled or semi-skilled workers, and are thus in greater danger of losing their jobs through automation. Since the passing of the Act in 1970, attempts have been made to bring in legislation to inhibit sex discrimination in education and employment in order to widen women's job opportunities. But the latest of these attempts, the Sex Discrimination (Removal) Bill, repeats the mistake of its ineffective predecessor, the Sex Disqualification (Removal) Act of 1919. This Act was not provided with adequate teeth. There are strong pressures on employers to evade legislation, like the Equal Pay Act, which makes women's work more expensive or like the Sex Discrimination Act, which questions deeply-felt if sketchily-based assumptions about women and work.

In the latter case, there is a backlog of outdated but rarely reassessed attitudes towards women. In essence, these reflect Victorian assumptions that woman's economic role is both secondary to and at odds with her social role as wife and mother. The opportunities for women to improve their own employment position are hampered by the difficulty of acquiring skills and promotion through training. Training schemes are all more readily available to men than to women and men find it far easier than women to persuade employers to allow them access to day-release and apprenticeship schemes.

The industries which discriminate most against women in this regard are those in which the largest numbers of women are employed. Government training centres for a long time concentrated on traditional men's work, offering courses in building and engineering. In response to criticism, attempts have been made to bring women into the fold. This was not done by persuading them to cross the old craft boundaries, which would have upset trade unions, but by offering extra courses in the overstocked female 'ghetto' occupations in clerical work and garment-making. On one estimate, the opportunities for women to do skilled work are actually decreasing, while the number of women in the work-force is rapidly increasing. Thus, it has been estimated, the number of women classed as skilled in industry fell by a third between 1911 and 1951, and a further $8\frac{1}{2}$ per cent by 1961.

The position is particularly bad so far as married women are concerned. While the number of men in the work-force is almost stationary, and that of women is rising, it is the number of married women that is rising fastest of all. These are mostly mothers who have finished having children, and have time to spare once their youngest child is at school. Whatever their skills when they left work such women share one characteristic on their return: they are out of touch with the latest techniques of their work.

As we shall see, this return to work of so many married women is connected with the trend towards earlier marriage, smaller families and labour-saving devices at home. Many want part-time work only, and in fact nearly a fifth of all women workers in manufacturing now work less than thirty hours a week, twice as many as twenty years ago. But the comparatively recent arrival of large numbers of married women in the labour market has not been matched by a commensurate expansion in part-time work or re-training.

The main areas of employment with a tradition of part-time work for women are in the distributive trades and miscellaneous services. But these also have a long history of low pay and poor working conditions. With few exceptions, the only employments which offer re-training are other usual ghetto occupations such as teaching and nursing. As a result, the onset of domestic responsibilities forces many married women to take a job which fits in with the other job of running a home, rather than one which matches their individual skills.

The availability of nursery places has fallen far behind the demand from mothers wishing to return to work. Married women, of whom less than half do paid work, are the only big remaining reserve of labour. Unless it is made easier for the other half to return to work, and unless better use is made of those who do return, this reserve will not be used to the full. The size of the labour force is expected to change little between now and 1980. One implication of this is that the burden of producing the wealth to support the non-employed population – the mother with young children, the old and the sick – is not to be more widely shared. Indeed, it is likelier to become heavier still, given our appetite for more and more goods and services.

Much has been written about 'the problem of leisure'. Are we, it is asked, ready for a world in which beneficent machines have removed the need for people to work long hours and for some people to work at all? There is, however, another problem that more nearly concerns us because it is here already. Machines are already able to do away with the jobs of unskilled workers without necessarily restoring either their self-respect or their financial loss. Since women workers are for the most part unskilled, they stand to lose the most on the way to the leisured society.

By the standards of half a century ago, the modern home is an outpost of that same society. The washing machine has replaced the copper, gas central heating has replaced the fire fed by coal heaved up from the cellar, and food is cooked on a clean, easily regulated gas stove instead of upon a grimy hob. The reaction of between a third and a half of the housewives to this new freedom is to go straight out and look for a job.

If our society continues to expect higher standards of living from a work-force that is hardly growing, then we cannot afford to have over a third of that work-force operating at levels of skill and of responsibility far below many of the individuals within it. Yet for three-quarters of this century, and all of the last, our society has misguidedly regarded women not as individuals but as members of a sex with uniform attributes, both physical and mental. Were this estimate of the sex not shared by so many of its own members, it would have been changed long ago. Yet from time to time throughout the last hundred years women have challenged the accepted bounds of their abilities. For instance, in the two world wars women saved the country's bacon by doing perfectly well all the jobs for which they had previously been regarded as unfit. And it is happening now, when activity rates for women – the percentage of the female population in certain age groups doing paid work – is higher than in 1943, at the height of the Second World War.

A 1968 government survey showed that the less skill women had, the happier they were with their work.

Possibly those with little or no skills settle happily into undemanding jobs, while those with more ability are dissatisfied with the limited opportunities open to them.[5]

However, non-manual women workers, whether in paid employment or not, ascribed greater importance to opportunities to use their qualifications than to any other factor, including high pay. Yet despite this, it is by no means certain that women realize, or concern themselves about, 'a situation . . . of inequality between men and women, in which generally women are the losers'.[6]

Women have been fully enfranchised since 1929, yet although they make up over half the population, the number who stand for Parliament has always been far less than half the total number of candidates. In the 1966 election for instance, eighty women stood, compared with 1627 men.

The number of women MPs elected at the 1970 General Election, twenty-six, was three fewer than in 1964. Moreover, those who have been elected have, with notable exceptions, either been slow to recognize the nature and seriousness of the employment position of women or have failed to agree on the means by which it might be bettered. Too often, the price of acceptance in the masculine world of politics has been to think and act along masculine lines, which in practice has meant overlooking the special problems of women. This in turn has helped divert the campaign for better treatment of working women from the area of common sense into that of radical politics, thus losing the potential support of many women. Only fourteen out of twenty-six women MPs attended a 1972 debate on an Anti-Discrimination Bill.

It is commonly assumed by employers that almost every young woman is a potential wife and mother. It is therefore not worth investing in training for her, according to this argument, for she will leave soon after marriage. The concept of working wives as earners of pin money, of wages merely supplementary to those of their husbands, has been used to justify low wages, where the lack of training renders such buttressing unnecessary. In the process, a great and growing wrong is being done to the thousands of women who do not fit into this tidy pattern.

It is true that many girls see the period between leaving school and marriage as merely an interlude for finding a

husband rather than acquiring a skill. It is true that for many
married women with children a job is merely a way of
earning some pocket money or of getting out of the house
and meeting people. However, it is no less true that there are
also thousands of women who do not have the backing of
a husband and his earnings. Nevertheless, such women must
still accept inferior pay and conditions of work as if they
had a second wage upon which to fall back. There are
widows, spinsters, unmarried mothers, deserted wives,
women supporting aged parents, all of whom are lumped
together in the labour market along with their more fortunate
sisters. Not for them individual treatment, such as a man
might reasonably expect. There are women's jobs at women's
rates with women's prospects, and that, for too long, has
been that.

But what of such jobs as women do have? We have already
seen that there have over the last twenty years been great
changes in the number and type of women in employment.
But these changes have yet to be complemented in conventional attitudes towards women at work. Most working
women, as we have noted, are concentrated in relatively
few accepted women's employments, and even within these
they frequently operate at low levels of training or of responsibility.

This restriction has for many years assured a fairly
plentiful supply of cheap female labour. This in turn has
guaranteed that, except in regions with particular employment problems, there are vacancies for such labour. One
effect of the availability of large amounts of this cheap
labour has been to delay the introduction of automation.
Another has been to produce a common response to low-
grade jobs where training is hard to get, namely, not to get
a higher-grade job but to switch from a low-grade job with
one employer to a low-grade job with another. And this
shifting about has been used, in a way symptomatic of our
whole approach to female employment, as a justification for

continuing to pay badly. Women, it is argued by employers, have a higher rate of turnover or of absenteeism than men. It rarely occurs to people that it is unskilled workers, which is what women tend to be, that have higher rates of absenteeism and turnover than skilled workers, whether they be men or women.

But women's labour is to be cheap no longer. On the first day of 1976 an Equal Pay Act comes into force. This requires that women should be paid the same basic rates as men where they are doing work that is the same or broadly similar or, where different, has been rated as of equal value by a job evaluation scheme. This is the first time a British government has seriously addressed itself to the problem of discrimination against women since it began to be discussed in the first half of the last century. In 1848 John Stuart Mill asked in *The Principles of Political Economy* 'Why the wages of women are generally lower, and very much lower, than those of men.' He came up with the answer that 'although so much smaller a number of women, than of men, support themselves by wages, the occupations which law and usage make accessible to them are comparatively so few, that the field of their employment is still more overcrowded'.

So far, however, we have progressed towards making women's work more expensive, without extending the range of jobs open to them. In fact, such jobs as women do have are being put at risk by the march of automation. About a third of the female work-force, for example, is employed in office work. This is an area where the computer waits in the wings, ready to gobble up jobs. Only the cheapness of clerical labour has so far restrained it.

Even in the professions women are on the retreat from beachheads established more than half a century ago. As more and more schools are merged into comprehensives, their headmistresses are finding that selection boards favour the male candidate. Personnel management, one of the newest professions, started during the last war as welfare work done primarily by women on behalf of other women drafted into the work-force to replace the men. Today, personnel management is an important part of any efficient enterprise. But as the status and the scope of the work have increased, so the men have taken over. Even where men and women are doing the same jobs, it is the men who command the higher salaries.

The situation described so far has lasted as long as it has partly because so many women are either ignorant of their plight or apathetic to it. But this is, of course, no justification for its continuance. Politicians, trade unionists and employers do not go around looking for wrongs to right. They react to pressure. Women, unfortunately, appear to have failed to recognize how unfavourable their treatment is. Or, where they have recognized the nature of their situation, they have been slow to organize and press for change. Now an Equal Pay Act is here at last, and anti-discrimination legislation is proposed to secure equal opportunities in recruitment, training and promotion. But Acts of Parliament do not in themselves banish abuses. On the contrary, they can lull people into the belief that more has changed than is really the case.

The Suffragists, for instance, expended their energies and in some cases their lives on securing the vote. But they failed to campaign vigorously enough to ensure that, once given, it was properly used. Meanwhile, fond mothers continue to bring up their daughters in the belief that some work is 'woman's work' and some only for men. This notion is remarkable for three things: its strength, the degree to which it is shared by both men and women, and the conviction that it has long been rooted in British tradition. It is into the truth of this assumption that we must now look.

2. Pre-industrial woman

You cannot expect to marry in such a manner as neither of you shall have occasion to work, and none but a fool will take a wife whose bread must be earned solely by his labour and who will contribute nothing towards it herself.

A Present for a Servant Maid, 1743

In 1750, on the eve of the Industrial Revolution, Britain was still primarily an agricultural country, much as in 1550 or 1250. What was the place of the female worker in that vanished society?

The importance of women to the economy of the nation as well as of the family was formally recognized as far back as medieval times when the Statute of Labourers of 1349 imposed upon women as upon men the obligation of working for the local magnate when required. The rates of pay which women could command were, however, pitched low enough to make full-time employment for women unattractive even where it was available. It has been argued that the fact that women throughout the centuries have in agriculture been paid less than men somehow constitutes a justification for the continuation of this principle in modern industrial society. The substance of this assumption is to be found in the following sort of evidence.

The Statute of 12, Richard II, 1388, states that 'because the wages of said labourers have not been put in certainty before these times, it is agreed that and assented that the bailiff of husbandry takes

13s. 4d. a year, and his clothing once a year at most, the master hind 10s., the cater 10s., the shepherd 10s., the oxherd 6s. 8d., the cowherd 6s. 8d., the swineherd 6s., the woman labourer 6s., the dairymaid 6s., the ploughman 7s. at most, and every other labourer and servant according to his degree.'[1]

Yet this view ignores the fundamental change in the employment situation of women before and since the Industrial Revolution, and indeed until the present day. The statutory obligation of women to turn out and work in the fields was a confirmation of the importance of women to an agrarian pre-industrial economy. But it served to make available that labour only in periods of great shortage. This might have been useful in the annual harvest, when the corn had to be gathered in quickly. But its origins lay in the Black Death of 1348–9, which reduced the population by about a third. Moreover, these women had to be forced into the labour market. There was a shortage of men to till the land, for so many had died. But many more, particularly those unencumbered with wives and children, left a particular demesne to avoid performing their workdays on the lord's land.

Often when the bailiff pressed a villein to perform his field-work he 'fled' to better himself on the other side of the forest, where every town and every village was so short of labour after the Black Death that high wages were given to migrants, and no questions asked as to whence they came.[2]

When the sanction of the law as defined by aristocratic self-interest was not so readily available, then more equitable considerations might prevail.

There are records between 1540 and 1582 of women harvesters being paid the same sums as their husbands. In general, however, the lower rate became the rule, as in an assessment at Oxford in 1605 that gave men haymakers 6d. and women 3d. But the essential difference between the situ-

ation of women in agrarian and industrial society was this:
in pre-industrial times a woman's labour in the fields was considered largely ancillary to her main duties in the home, which
might include not only looking after the house, and the
kitchen garden, but also the cottage industries of weaving or
spinning. In industrial society, a woman's duties at home often
took second place to her work in the mill or at the pit. Not
until 1844 were the hours of women limited to twelve a day
and then only in textile factories. Her wage, traditionally set
lower than a man's now became the hammer by which the
man's wage could be driven down. This was a far cry from
casual seasonal work; it was rather a full-time struggle to
avoid starvation during times when over-production, the
chronic disease of the early industrial system, drove manufacturers to keep down prices by cutting wages.

Yet for all their differences the jobs allocated to women
in the industrial system mirrored their duties in the agrarian
period. Even today, except for the minority who are employed
in the technology-based industries of computers and elec-
tronics, most women still work within a very familiar pattern
of employment. The occupations of nurses, teachers and
social workers are only the modern embodiment of the
ancient role of women as the bringers-up of children. Equally
significant is the great concentration of female workers in
the fields of textiles, clothing and footwear, and in food,
drink and tobacco. There is a clear link between these
employments and the role of women in the home as preparers
of food and makers of clothing.

The differential between men's and women's work in the
pre-industrial economy was in a sense a protection to both:
it discouraged unattached women from taking work from
men by undercutting them; and it upheld the importance of
women's work in the home, which contributed as much as
'outwork' to the family economy, if not more. What, then,
was this work at home?

For a farm labourer and his wife, the modern distinction

between the privacy of home and the bustle of work did not apply. Home was very much a workplace. It had to be. A labourer hired himself out for a fixed wage that was so calculated as to be enough only to maintain himself. His wife and his children were expected to maintain themselves as best they might. Household duties involved more than today's tasks of washing, cleaning and cooking. They included providing and preserving, as well as cooking, the family's food.

Women were required to tend a garden patch, orchard, poultry, pig or calf. Milk and cheese from the family cow, if a labourer was lucky enough to own one, would also be used to earn money to pay for the few things such a family would provide for itself. Inside the house, there was the bread to bake, beer to brew, and soap or candles to make. There would also be some form of domestic industry, be it spinning, weaving or lace-making. Where such work was not available, then other work, any work, had to be sought outside the home.

As servants in husbandry, women performed the heaviest kinds of agricultural labour; they served as assistants to masons and bricklayers, as labourers in brickyards, and foundries, as load carriers to and from markets, as rag sorters and cutters in paper mills, as cinder shifters and collectors of refuse.[3]

In the towns, the women of a merchant's or craftsman's family worked in the family business, although for little or no wage. Furthermore, the more skilled and organized the trade, the stronger the constraints upon what women and girls were allowed to do. The London Weavers' Ordinance of 1596 laid down that 'no woman or mayd shall use or exercise the Arts of weaving . . . except she be the widow of one of the same Guild.' The reason was obvious enough.

The London Weavers' Company's traditional attitude to the

employment of women as weavers is naturally linked with its restrictive regulations on the teaching of the craft, for in the absence of strict control on the latter, women and maids could have been taught, with little difficulty, all but the most skilled branches of weaving.[4]

One wonders, incidentally, why women's abilities stopped short of 'the highest branches' of weaving. The London weavers followed through this policy with some vigour, although not all were in agreement especially those who wanted to use the cheap female labour. In 1653, for example, John Higg was found to be employing a girl as a weaver 'for which the company ordered him to discharge the wench forthwith, and if after she got work by his means upon any woven work then he pay £5 to the Company'.

Women could be put to work in ancillary functions. An early factory was described as

> ... one room being large and long
> [where] stood two hundred looms full strong,
> Two hundred men the truth is so
> wrought in all those looms in a row.[5]

'Pretty boys' did the quilling, while the carding and spinning were performed by

> an hundred women merily ...
> And in a chamber close beside,
> Two hundred maidens did abide ...

A wife, however, was regarded as a partner in trade, and a widow could take over all the rights, privileges and liabilities of her husband. But if a London weaver's widow remarried she, unlike a stationer's widow, was forbidden to add her looms, journeymen and apprentices to those of her new husband. Similarly, a non-weaver who married a weaver's widow could be prosecuted for carrying on the trade

Widow Goodale 'gave bad words' to the Company when in 1667 she was asked to give up weaving.

In good times the system worked well enough. Women worked within the framework of the family: their contribution, whether in domestic work, in food grown or goods sold, was supplementary to the men's earnings. By and large, women as workers were unwilling or unable to compete with men. Their pay outside the home was in any case not high enough to tempt many to do so.

The money earned thereby would hardly balance the cost of the loss of services to the family. However, this system, which had lasted so long, was in the last resort seen to be based on one and only one foundation: that the supply of labour, notably men's labour, was enough to meet the demands of agriculture and of industry. Without that the whole edifice began to sag.

This is precisely what happened. The Industrial Revolution upset the whole balance of supply and demand in the labour market in a way that even now we are just beginning to set right. As the demand for labour mushroomed in the expanding mining and textile industries women and children poured in.

But by the nature of their former employments they were less fitted than the men to secure the best return for their efforts. Often they worked not directly for the owner but for the hands he employed. As helpers in the old domestic industry, their labour had been cheap. Because they could make themselves useful in so many ways without necessarily learning any one skill in depth, their training tended to be slight. Their very usefulness kept them from needing to acquire any but the most basic skills.

The combination of a lack of negotiable skills and the inability to acquire new skills outside led women to cluster in a narrow range of industries most closely related to the type of work done in the home. The ensuing glut in the female labour market, and the exclusion of women from the ranks of skilled and organized labour, gave apparent sanction to the pre-industrial tradition that a woman's wage should rightly be less than that of a man.

Even before the great changes, the system operated to the benefit of women only so long as they were protected by the superior earnings of the male. But what happened if the husband or father died? What of a woman thrown upon her own resources, who had to live on the lower, woman's wage appropriate not to her new position but that of a wife working in partnership with her husband? Her commitments, if she had children or aged relatives, might not be less. In relation to reduction of income caused by the loss of her husband, they in fact became proportionately higher. Thus she was thrown upon a crowded market where the price of her labour, by custom low, was now depressed yet further.

How a woman fared, therefore, lay not so much in her willingness to work as in her luck in finding it. It did not even depend primarily upon her skill. More women might expect to work at a trade in the town than in the country. Yet it was in the town that the effects of unemployment were the more deeply felt.

In 1752 Henry Fielding, the author of *Tom Jones* and a Bow Street magistrate, remarked on the high incidence of suicide among women: 'For hardly a week passes without one or more of that kind, and few or no men have been for some time known to have committed the crime. Perhaps the distress to which some females have been lately reduced may in some measure account for it.'[6]

In 1763, a housebuyer inspecting a property in Stonecutter Street (off Fleet Street) found in two rooms three women dead and two others nearly dead from starvation. Two had been working as porters in a nearby market.

In the country, so long as the handicraft and domestic system withstood the factory and the mill, women worked unpaid in the home. The only regular employment for single women outside their home was in somebody else's – in domestic service.

B

This employment was therefore overstocked and those who could not get or could not stay in such work were forced either to rely on casual spinning or manual work on the farms. Others fled to the towns, there to swell further the ranks of unemployed women. For many, it was the way to Gin Street or to the knocking shop.

Meanwhile, in some parts of the country women had been employed in industry, sometimes in heavy industry, long before the Industrial Revolution. In the Birmingham area women and children worked at home making up (at piece-work rates) toys, jewellery, pins and needles. In the Thames Valley they made baskets, and in Stafford and Worcester nails and chains. In 1322, Emma, daughter of William Culchaxe, was killed by 'le Damp' in a 'colepyt' at Morley, Derbyshire. In remote coalmining areas where there might be a shortage of men, women were not only permitted to work the pits, they could be forced to. In Scotland until 1799 men, women and children working in the mines became serfs, forbidden to leave the collier's employment under 'pain of punishment in their bodies'. Women also worked in metal mining. In 1699 one observer noted: 'There is washing and knocking of ores, which are the works that many good men's daughters are now glad to do, in many places in this Kingdom, for bread for them and their children.'

Woolmaking, before the Industrial Revolution the busiest British industry, was carried on in the home. The provision of clothing had been a duty of women from earlier times and, accordingly, women were widely employed in this home industry. In the fourteenth and fifteenth centuries they worked as wool-sorters, warpers, carders, spinners, dyers and weavers. However, as early as the fifteenth century, the woollen industry was being transferred from the homes of the workers to the workshops of capitalist clothiers. There the men became the weavers in the workshops, while the thread was spun by the women working at home. Sometimes the yarn was delivered to their door, but often the luckless women had to trudge for miles along what then passed for roads to collect it.

Cotton, which became, along with steelmaking, the growth industry of the Industrial Revolution, was originally a very minor manufacture. This again was a cottage industry, although the man of the house normally either did the weaving himself or superintended it. His wife and children would pick and clean the cotton, as well as doing the washing, carding and spinning.

Lacemaking was another matter. 'The Lace Manufacture of England is the greatest, next to woolen . . . and the persons employed at it are, for the most part, women and children who have no other means of subsistence', claimed a petition of the lace manufacturing trade to Parliament in 1699. In the silk industry, the Spitalfields weavers put children over seven out to hire. The customer could take his pick every Tuesday and Monday from the children's market in Bethnal Green.

Women, it is clear, were therefore engaged in productive work in agriculture and in industry long before the Industrial Revolution. Their work was largely subsidiary to that done by men. They were paid poorly, and often not at all. They did not have the legal right to possess their own earnings. But an industrious wife was an asset. She had a standing and an economic existence that derived from her role in helping out the family's earnings, not in competition but in co-operation with her husband and with other men working in the same line. It was not to last. The Industrial Revolution was gradually to draw the weaving, first of wool, and secondly of cotton, away from the home and into the mill. The demands of the mills and the factories grew fast, first for labour and then, with the recurrent crisis of capitalist over-production, for cheap labour.

This then was to be the new function of female labour. In this competition with the interests of male workers, there was a clear break with the past, a break that is only now beginning to heal. Not that the time before the mills and the factories was a Golden Age. As we have seen, high death rates created widows and orphans, dissolving arbitrarily the family units around which work was carried on. Even when the family worked together, the combination of workshop and roofed farmyard that characterized rural labourers' homes was not conducive to health, comfort or cleanliness. The cottage of a weaver, unless he was in a substantial way of business, would be cluttered with spinning wheel, loom wool being prepared for use, unwoven yarn, raw material arrived from the clothier, and parcels of made-up yarn or cloth due for return to him. On top of this, there was bread to be baked and beer to be brewed, and this all had to be done in what hours were left from paid labour. In short, what with the whine of the shuttle, the fluff and the grease of the wool, the presence of livestock wandering in and out, and the overcrowded conditions of the household, home was no paradise.

Until the end of the eighteenth century many of these homes were built of mud. Weavers often favoured damp situations because this made the thread less likely to snap. There were few cooking utensils. Food was usually limited to oatmeal porridge, milk, bread, cheese and potatoes. Turf and furze were until late in the eighteenth century the principal fuels. In such circumstances, a woman trained in domestic service was valued as a wife by working men because she would have had some experience of the conditions in bigger houses, and would therefore be better equipped to make a home out of the chaos around her.

Nevertheless, such a way of life had its positive side, implying a family co-operation based upon the mutual respect that came of clearly defined functions. But change was on the way. The pace of enclosure of common land quickened as the eighteenth century wore on and as the landowners sought to increase their holdings in order to make use of the latest developments in agriculture.

By the beginning of the 1700s the British iron industry was in decline due to shortages of charcoal, the fuel then used for smelting. In 1709, however, Abraham Darby succeeded in using coke to smelt iron good enough for casting. In 1720 Newcomen developed a steam pump which, when perfected, brought back into production coal mines previously rendered unworkable by flooding. John Kay in 1733 invented a fly-shuttle that enormously increased the speed of weaving. Shortly afterwards, Hargreaves invented the 'Spinning Jenny' which did for spinning what Kay's fly-shuttle had done for weaving. During the last ten years of the eighteenth century it became possible to smelt iron with ordinary coal, one of the country's most abundant resources, while Whitney developed a cotton gin which enabled Britain to use the produce of the vast cottonfields of the United States.

By 1814 the value of cotton manufacture had surpassed that of wool. By this time, too, Watt's method of powering a mill by steam made it possible to maintain a longer period of continuous work than with waterpower, when a certain time was lost while water was brought in from the reservoir upstream. By 1815 the handloom was becoming an unprofitable method of cotton manufacture, and the stage was set for the slow and pitiful death of the domestic system. The factory and the mill offered work, while, in the agricultural districts, the landlords were knocking down cottages to create bigger and more factory-like farms. Gradually, women had to follow their traditional 'outwork' as it was first cheapened and then withdrawn from the home and relocated in the mills or the factory. When they got there, what sort of bargain could they strike, given their previous background?

3. The Industrial Revolution

Nature effects her own purpose wisely and more effectively than could be done by the wisest of men. The low price of female labour makes it the most profitable as well as the most agreeable occupation for a female to superintend her own domestic establishment and her low wages do not tempt her to abandon the care of her own children.

Supplementary Report on Child Labour in Factories, 1844

They are also less disposed than men to combine for the purpose of extorting higher wages, and this is by no means an unimportant matter.

Report to Postmaster-General, 1871

Few men before the beginning of the last century would have been willing or able to marry a woman solely because he found her sexually attractive. That they began to do so came about as the result of the great changes in economic life that had begun about a century before, and whose main guidelines were now set. The British Isles had changed from being primarily an agricultural to primarily an industrial nation. By the 1850s the inventions of the preceding century in steampower, in steelmaking and textiles were fully developed and fully employed.

For some they created vast fortunes. For many more it became possible to lead a home life more like that of their social superiors. The new wealth had made merchants of shopkeepers and manufacturers of workmen. Riches and the spread of the railways enabled such people not only to live in some style but also, perhaps for the first time, to make a home away from the scene of their labours. A century before, the shopkeeper lived above his shop. The successful merchant or manufacturer now sought a home away from the forge or the counting-house.

The less well-off carried away their wives and daughters to bowers among the widening swathes of suburban villas. Above all, such men sought to express their wealth and developing power first through the finery and then through the idleness of their women. To a degree this made a virtue of necessity, since the women, like the men, were isolated from the place of work. Lastly, upheavals in the countryside, as we shall see, provided an inexhaustible supply of domestic servants.

This spiritual and physical isolation from work marked a break with the past, and the beginning of a new and perhaps less honourable tradition. In the previous history of these islands, women had performed a role that was complementary rather than secondary to that as propagator of children, that of a producer rather than a consumer of the wealth of the family and of the nation. To take a woman for adornment's sake may have been the humour of the aristocracy, but for that class it was the profession of the man as well as of the woman to be idle. Even if such a wife were expected neither to spin nor sew, she was none the less required to bring with her land, gold or title.

The Industrial Revolution caused men and later women to be herded in their thousands into factories where they worked long hours when work was available. In the frequent periods of industrial over-production, starvation was an ever-present reality. Weavers in their homes constantly sought to cheapen their labour to stave off the day when their work would be done on power looms in the new mills. The men now in the factories were not strangers to squalor, starvation and early death. But the revolutionary new machines eroded many of the old freedoms.

Formerly in Cornwall the miner on his descent into the mine had begun by sleeping as long as it takes a candle to burn down. He had then worked for two or three hours, at the conclusion of which he rested for half an hour to smoke a pipe before recommencing work. Half the day had been spent in sleeping and lounging about.[1]

By the beginning of the nineteenth century this was no longer possible. Such was the demand for coal that narrow seams and flooded shafts, once considered unworkable, were reopened with the aid of power pumps and steam engines to take the coal away from the mine. The capital required was high, and the men were driven harder to keep up the owners' profits. As the increasing demand for iron and coal drew more labour into mining, so each lay-off or wage-cutting due to periodic over-production hurt more men and, inevitably, more women.

Sometimes women's sufferings were even more direct. Women and girls had long been employed in mines, particularly in Scotland, the women to lead the horses that hauled the laden carts away from the pithead, the girls to open and shut gates for them. 'The management of the mine left the payment of the women and children to the miners, together with the full liberty to use them at pleasure for the gratification of their bestial and filthy desires.'[2]

But the enduring legacy of the Industrial Revolution was not so much the brutalization of the labouring class as the severing of the partnership in work between the sexes. In the cotton industry for instance, the foremost growth area of that time, this community of interest was sundered by the influx of large numbers of women. One or even more of the new machines could be operated by a single skilled man, but numbers of unskilled women or children were required simply to 'watch' the machine. The newcomers could be paid less than unskilled men for doing the same job, and as a consequence many men were displaced. Of 10 000 workers employed in forty-one Scottish mills in 1816, two-thirds were female, many of them children below eighteen.[3]

In forty-eight Manchester mills there were twice as many women as men, and as many children as adults. Nor might some mills be any less unpleasant for women than the mines. In 1828, the Radical Francis Place told a French traveller that when a friend visited a Lancashire mill, the owner invited him to have his choice of the mill girls. The low wages both here and in the mushrooming cities were regularly supplemented by prostitution.

In Manchester an almost promiscuous intercourse prevails in the great mass of the people, in so much that the magistrates attempt to check the increase of bastard children by inflicting stripes and imprisonment on the women who bear above a certain number.[4]

Where and when work was plentiful, something like the old compact remained.

It must be remembered that father, mother, son and daughter are alike engaged; no one capable of working is spared to make home (to which, after a day of such toil and privation, they are hastening) comfortable and desirable.[5]

But it was a sad sort of co-operation, for, if the mill fell idle, the whole family would be without work and therefore without wages. And this time, living in a back-to-back terraced slum, there was, of course, no kitchen garden.

The industrial system set one man's wife or daughter against another woman's father or husband in the mill towns. Yet the rivalry for this new work was ironic, since much of the work in the woollen and cotton industries had originally been 'women's work'. This is why an unmarried woman was a 'spinster'. Long before the Industrial Revolution, spinning had been the sure way an unsupported woman might make some contribution to her keep. The good housewife, we are told in 1540, sought to 'let the distaff be always ready for a pastyme'.

As the picking, cleaning and weaving of cotton became increasingly concentrated in the factories, the work at first was a male prerogative. But gradually women and children were substituted as machinery improved. In one way, of course, women were only reasserting a claim to work that had once been theirs: but it was a claim made against a background of privation, sweated labour and deepening antipathy between men and women workers.

In agricultural districts, the change-over from female to male wool spinners had been achieved with similar suffering. Initially, the spinning was done on heavy 'mules' which needed men to operate them. In the 1830s, parishes told the Poor Law Commissioners that 'formerly all the women and children had spinning to do, and they brought in as much as the men did; but now there is no employment but field-work'. It was from the ranks of the dispossessed female wool spinners that the cotton spinners were found, misery thus feeding upon itself.

Mr E, a manufacturer, informed us that he employs females exclusively on the power looms, especially those who have families at home dependent on them for support; they are attentive, doubly more so than unmarried women and are compelled to use their utmost exertions to procure the necessities of life.[6]

Men often resented bitterly the way that the newer machinery enabled more work to be done by women, at lower rates. A silk weaver in the 1840s wrote:

When I had served about three years of my apprenticeship, a serious riot occurred among the weavers during a strike. A loom, very much larger than the ordinary one, had been invented by Mr Josiah Beck, to be worked by steam power. He had already filled a large building with these looms and employed young women at weekly wages to manage them. This was entirely against the usages of the trade, as the weavers had always opposed female labour in the actual making of ribbons and only employed women as subsidiary helps. The proposed reductions in the price of labour and the introduction of steam power, incensed the weavers to such an extent that the town was soon in a state of ferment and uproar.[7]

The outcome of this particular riot, in which the looms were smashed, was the transportation of three men. The hapless Mr Beck, however, escaped the fury of the mob, who 'had the determination of subjecting the proprietor to the indignity of riding on a donkey through the streets tailwards . . . a common punishment for those who had transgressed any usage of the various trades in Coventry'. The three transported Luddites later returned from Australia as rich men.

However, neither the action of the mob, nor of the trade unions could halt the steady influx of cheap female labour. So it was that although more and more women came into the industrial economy, they did so without the safety of numbers. Most men, equating female labour with downward pressure on wage rates, if not the loss of the job itself, formed themselves into exclusively male trade unions. Such protection as women could get came not from organization and from collective bargaining but from legislation as middle-class consciences were aroused by their sufferings.

Being externally imposed, however, attempts to mitigate this suffering of working women often ignored the fact that the work, harsh though it was, was badly needed. There might be no other work to go to, especially in rural areas. The Mines Act of 1842, for example, forbade the employment of women and girls underground. But:

The women who were turned out of the pits had, in many districts, no alternative employment, and serious distress followed the loss of their occupation. The worst cases occurred in Scotland, where the mining population was more isolated than in England from the rest of the community. The women affected in Scotland numbered 2400. Some of them tried to get back into pits disguised as men.[8]

Yet the conditions of women in the mines were especially bad. The Factory Commission of 1833 had heard the testimony of Betty Harris, a woman of thirty-seven who worked as a drawer at Little Bolton pit, where she hauled trucks of coal through the passages by means of a girdle and chain.

I have a belt round my waist and a chain passing between my legs and I go on my hands and feet. The road is steep and we have to hold by a rope, and when there is no rope, by anything we can catch hold of. . . . The pit is very wet where I work and the water comes over our clog-tops always and I have seen it up to my thighs; it rains in at the roof terribly, my clothes are wet through almost all day long. . . . I have drawn till I have had the skin off me; the belt and chain is worse when we are in the family way.[9]

The first effective Factory Act was passed in 1833. It applied only to textile mills, and forbade the employment of children under nine, and regulated hours of work. In 1844, this was extended to include women. Throughout the century controls over the working conditions of women and of children were gradually extended over a wider range of manufacturing industry, although it was not until 1901 and the Factory and Workshop Act that these controls were combined with sections dealing with health, safety and the education of children. Yet even today, incidentally, this protection still extends to less than one in four working women.

Improvements of factory conditions through legislation throughout the last century was not only slow, but also on a narrow front. There grew up in the new industrial towns, and particularly in London, a whole range of 'sweated' industries, brought into being to take advantage of the availability of cheap female labour. The miserable conditions of these sweated workers were anticipated by the home-based wool and cotton spinners of Yorkshire and Lancashire, whose earnings were frequently reduced, either through arbitrary wage cuts by their employers or through fines imposed for allegedly sloppy work.

London had traditionally been a city of small workshops, catering to the luxury trade of millinery, haberdashery, tailoring and jewellery. The men of the capital also had a tradition of political activism going back to the peasant risings of the Middle Ages, and throughout the last half of the eighteenth century the city was a hive of radical trade union activity. But there was also a vast army of women with no such tradition, only too glad to work at home or in dingy workrooms, doing the dirty work that lay behind the elegant windows of the furriers and dress-shops of Piccadilly.

The inquirer who turns aside out of that historic street from which one April day there started long ago a famous and jocund company of pilgrims – where today a sadder stream of humanity ceaselessly ebbs and flows – and who plunges under one of the narrow archways on its western side, will find himself face to face with the lowest depths to which the toil of women can be dragged.

At first the women are suspicious. They imagine you are an emissary of the London County Council – in their eyes, the embodiment of unlimited and tyrannical power. The County Council and the law are their standing dread; for if they take it upon them to interfere and deprive the 'fur-puller' of her employment, there is nothing left but starvation.

It is the business of the fur-puller, broadly speaking, to remove the long coarse hairs from rabbit skins . . . the countless miscellaneous odours of the alley are absorbed in one which overpowers the rest – the sickly, unmistakable smell of uncleaned skins. On entering the house the air becomes thick with millions of almost impalpable hairs which float in it . . . the window is tightly closed, because such air as can find its way in from the stifling court below would force the hairs into the noses and eyes and lungs of the workers.

The two prematurely aged women – whose unkempt matted hair is almost hidden with a thick covering of fluff, whose clothing is of the scantiest, seeming to consist of bits of sacking fashioned into some semblance of garments – are sitting on low stools before a roughly made deal trough, into which they throw the long upper hairs of the skin . . . which is afterwards manufactured into felt hats.

The heaps of skins by their side are dried, but uncleaned, and still covered with congealed blood. What do they get from it? They each of them say they can pull a 'turn and a half' working 12 hours. A 'turn' means 60 skins, and the rate of pay is 11d. – per 'turn' – 1s. 4½d. for the 12 hours. The pulled out hair is carefully selected and weighed at the shop, a turn being supposed to yield two pounds. If the turn is deficient in quantity, the value is, at some factories, deducted from the price of the work.[10]

The impact of the Industrial Revolution was not confined to the towns. As the population of England and Wales rose from about 7 million in 1760 to over 9 million in 1801, the year of the first official census, agriculture could no longer provide enough corn to feed the numbers. At the same time, therefore, as entrepreneurial weavers were establishing mills along the Pennine streams of Lancashire and Yorkshire, the landed gentry were calculating the profits to be made from the new scientific methods in agriculture.

The great landowners of the day began to speed up the enclosure of open fields and commons. In the arable areas of the east, north-east and east midlands, the seized land was used to grow corn; in East Anglia, vegetables. As the landowners were the majority in Parliament, they could not only enclose common lands, but could usually arrange matters so that they also set the terms for the villagers' compensation. At first, this meant a temporary increase in work for male and female labourers, since there was fencing and hedging to be done, while the land had to be divided and drained. But once this was done, the villagers had either to seek work in the towns with their new factories, or face an uncertain future, bereft of their land and livestock, and living on casual labouring and spinning and weaving – in competition with the new machinery.

At the beginning of the nineteenth century the wages of agricultural labourers had been subsidized from the rates in line with fluctuations in the price of corn. But the Poor Law of 1834 abolished this subsidy, known as 'outdoor relief'. Henceforth, women and children were increasingly forced out of the home to seek work such as seasonal labour in the fields or stone-breaking on the roads.

Rural employers were content to put the new labourers to work for a number of reasons. First it kept the families out of the 'Bastilles' (the new workhouses that had replaced outdoor relief) and therefore held down the 'poor rates' at a low level. Secondly, the extra labour enabled the wages to be kept down, a fact which did not sink in with the married men immediately, since they had never worked for a wage big enough to support a whole family. However, single men soon found that their place was being taken by families who otherwise would be a heavier charge upon the rates. With the gang systems which grew up in the eastern counties, we see the new 'scientific' agriculture in full flower. The enclosed estates needed occasional labour on a large scale, although no labourers might now live nearby, their cottages having been pulled down. These were the 'closed parishes' where settlement was not allowed.

Elsewhere, in the adjacent 'open parishes', there sprang up a race of gang-masters willing to exploit the opposite situation, where there were too many labourers for the work to be found on the land that lay nearby. The gang-master would contract to a farmer to do a particular job for a particular sum, and would then recruit women and children to do the work. Of course, for them, the system involved not only hard work for whatever sum the gang-master cared to

pay, but also long walks to the empty lands where the work
was to be done. A father of an eleven-year-old girl said
in 1843:

I'm forced to let my daughter go, else I'm very much against
it . . . she has complained of pain in her side very often; they drive
them along, force them along – they make them work very hard.
Gathering stones has hurt my girl's back at times. Pulling turnips
is the hardest work . . . it blisters their hands so they can hardly
touch anything . . . my girl went five miles yesterday to her work,
turniping; she got off between seven and eight; she walked, had
a piece of bread before she went; she did not stop work in the
middle of the day; ate nothing till she left off; she came home
between three and four o'clock. Their walks are worse than their
work; she is sometimes so tired, she can't eat no victuals when
she comes home.[11]

The system was condemned almost from the outset, but
was not finally ended until 1876 with the passage of an
Education Act which forbade the employment of children
under ten in agriculture. But by that time, in agriculture as in
industry, the harmony of interest between men and women
in their work had been broken. Women, even children, were
driven to slave for their very existence, only to be resented
by men as a drag on wages and a constant threat, held in
reserve by the employers, should men become too active
in the pursuit of a fairer share of the fruits of their labours.

Yet there is another side to the picture. The frame of
common interest had been smashed, but it is doubtful whether
unindustrialized agriculture could have fed the millions of
new mouths. The fact that women were forced to take work
in mills, factories and fields was not only an indication of a
switch but of an increase in the demand for female labour.

For the first time, therefore, women could in large numbers
achieve the independence that came from financial self-
sufficiency. In the towns, girls were by 1833 already able to
leave home at the age of sixteen if their parents refused to

allow them to keep their own wages and pay a fixed sum for board.

One of the greatest advantages resulting from the progress of manufacturing industry and from severe manual labour being superseded by machinery is its tendency to raise the condition of women. . . .

But this independence vanished on marriage, since not until the Married Women's Property Act of 1921 did women retain a legal right to their earnings. The continual pregnancies and shorter life expectation of those times saw to it that this brief spell of freedom was soon over. Was this short interlude worth the shattering of the community of interest? For the truth was that women were hired only because they were cheap and plentiful and therefore unorganized and docile.

Early in the last century, power began to pass rapidly from the landed aristocracy into the hands of the new mercantile and industrial middle class. This transfer of power brought some gains to other classes as well. For example, repeal of the Combination Acts in 1824 gave working people the right to form associations or trade unions. The Catholic Emancipation Act of 1829 extended religious liberty to Catholics, who until this time were debarred from attending university or from holding government office. In 1832, the Reform Act gave the vote to a larger proportion of the male, but not the female, population

Before the Reform Act women had not voted: but then neither had most men. Legal opinion was divided as to women's rights in the matter. Now custom was given statutory sanction by two of the reformers' earliest measures, the Reform Act of 1832 and the Municipal Corporations Act of three years later. Women had not voted. Henceforth they could not. Thus among the first deeds of a liberal, reforming age was the legal limitation of women's rights. Why should this be? It seems as if the new ideas of freedom, of equality and of the development of human potentiality were thought applicable to men only.

Regarded as mentally and physically inferior to man, woman was, by her very nature, held to be incapable of leading the varied life of man, incapable of assuming his responsibilities or enjoying his opportunities. She was frail, easily influenced, foolish, requiring his protection, not only against an inclement world but also against her own weakness, not only in her own interest but also in the interest of man.[12]

The idea of women as 'the weaker sex', so attractive to the eighteenth-century philosophers such as Rousseau, was further fuelled by economic changes taking place as the old century gave way to the new.

Until comparatively recent times, the only way a women of the comfortable classes could achieve financial security and social status was to marry, and thus consign herself wholly to her husband. For a married woman was to all intents and purposes in a state of civil death: until 1882 she did not exist under the law. Unless she had entered into a contract before marriage, everything she owned as a single woman became her husband's. Until early in the last century a man could still sell his wife. *The Times* actually wrote that 'the increasing value of the fair sex is regarded by many writers as the certain index of growing civilization'.

Thus working life for a woman ended with marriage. Among the well-to-do there was, of course, no working life even before marriage. Many wives preferred it that way. Society had so conditioned them that they lacked the confidence or the training to shift for themselves. There was nevertheless a strong undercurrent of protest among women of mettle. In 1852, two years before she set off for the Crimea, Florence Nightingale described a day in the life of a young woman (herself) in a well-to-do home. The morning is spent 'sitting around a table in the drawing room, looking at prints, doing worsted work and reading little books'. In the afternoon, she took 'a little drive'. When night came, she wrote, women 'suffer – even physically . . . the accumulation of nervous energy, which has had nothing to do during the day, makes them feel every night, when they go to bed, as if they were going mad'.[13]

Many women suffered more directly. Although the only secure career was marriage, for demographic reasons a quarter of women were doomed not to marry. Even among the well-to-do, so limited was the education and training of women that about the only career open to them was that of governess, which in consequence became badly overstocked and thus poorly paid. In old age their position was often extreme. Lower down the social scale, the results were felt sooner and more harshly. Here, women had always worked, but usually as assistants to their fathers or their husbands.

'Because their labour was subsidiary,' writes Ivy Pinchbeck, 'it was cheap, and because they could perform useful service in many ways without technical training, they were often denied apprenticeship and the rank of skilled workers.'[14]

So long as a married woman was contributing to or benefiting from a family wage, life might go on with dignity and, by the standards of the time, comfort. As soon as women became dependent upon their own efforts, however, the falseness of their position became apparent.

Spinsters, deserted wives, widows and unmarried mothers with children to support could expect a rough passage. Parish records in country districts showed many women vagrants among those who received temporary or regular doles. In the towns, more women were brought up to a trade, but the numbers looking for domestic work were swollen by the refugees from the countryside. The result was that many were driven to prostitution or to suicide. By the middle of the last century the status of woman as a dependant had been established and was sanctified by custom and by law. The status has since been modified but not changed. Such legislation as has been passed has served to protect women in the narrow range of employment into which they are confined, rather than to extend the employments to which they might aspire.

4. Trade unions: men only

She was amazed to find herself the only female delegate in attendance when there were so many toilers of her own sex.
Margaret Bondfield at 1899 TUC Congress

In 1778 when the spinning wheel was being replaced by machinery, a Sisterhood of Hand Spinners at Leicester petitioned Parliament against the factory system in the following terms:

The business of spinning in all its branches hath ever been time out of mind the peculiar employment of women; insomuch that every single woman is called in law a spinster . . . it is with great concern your petitioners see that this ancient employment is likely to be taken from them. . . . This we apprehend will be the consequence of so many spinning mills, now erecting after the model of cotton mills.[1]

Since the first machines were cumbersome men were employed to work them, and soon monopolized the trade. In time, however, power looms were developed, and women once again became weavers. But by now they were such a disadvantaged section of the work-force that they had to accept such terms as they could get.

Here we see for the first time the economic interests of women brought into conflict with those of men. There followed throughout the first half of the nineteenth century a stout rearguard action by male workers, in which two of the main weapons were machine-wrecking and the trade union. Women workers had become an extension of the

bosses' self-interest and therefore victims rather than bene-
ficiaries of trade union militancy. The faster the pace of
technological improvement, the faster were machines able
to break down complex operations, thus allowing in even
more women workers and stiffening male trade unionists'
resolve to make life awkward for them. In 1795, for example,
the Manchester Spinners' Society allowed women into
membership. But when in 1829 a Grand General Union of
Spinners in the United Kingdom was formed, a resolution
was adopted 'that the union shall include only male spinners
and piecers'.

In Scotland there were bitter struggles to keep out under-
paid, underorganized women and children from spinning-
rooms. Earlier, women and children had only been used in
the textile mills in areas where there was a shortage of men;
now they were being preferred to men. Had trade unionism
been allowed to develop freely as the last century began, men
workers might have been able to absorb women into their
unions, and to use their combined strength to stop employers
from undercutting male wage rates.

The ruling landed class had little sympathy for the new
race of low-born mill-owners of the north. But their distaste
was weaker than their fear of the contagion of the French
Revolution, and the suspicion that unions might provide a
rallying point for political rather than industrial disaffection.
The Combination Acts of 1799 and 1800 restricted the
organization of working people. Although the penalty was
only three months' imprisonment, a nervous ruling class
could invoke through the magistrates' bench the far vaguer
yet much more serious offence of conspiracy. Clandestine
union activity of a sort survived despite trials, *agents
provocateurs* and public whippings. It was strongest in
the textile trades, since these had been the first to become
industrialized.

It was at this time, however, that women were becoming
available and sought after for millwork, a time when union

activity was discouraged, when male organizations distrusted women, while the women themselves, fresh from generations of working at home, had no tradition of combination. The 'docility' so much prized by employers was to a degree born of their newly won extremely tenuous position in the market place. In 1808, for instance, there were strikes in which the women were 'if possible more turbulent and mischievous than the men'. In 1824, the year of the repeal of the Combination Acts, eleven men and twelve women weavers were haled before a magistrate for refusing to have up to 9d. a week docked from their wages in payment for artificial light. They were sent for a walk in the yard, during which they could make up their minds either to pay up or to be locked up. The men and the women chose to go to prison, and duly got a month.

On repeal of the Combination Acts, many weaving unions voted to exclude women, and it is from then on that the principle of two separate labour markets, one for men and one for women, was institutionalized as a fact of British industrial life. The story of women's involvement in trade unionism from now for nearly another century is largely that of separate development, with few women to be found in male trade unions and vice versa.

In contrast with the men's unions, women's organizations were largely ineffective. They produced some outstanding individual leaders, but in the end were unable even to secure equal pay for those women doing the same jobs as men. Small and financially weak, women's unions could rarely bring pressure successfully to bear at industry level, although there were occasional successes against individual employers. However, even had women been brought into men's unions in any great number, it is unlikely that this would have had much effect in improving the conditions under which they worked in the first half of the last century. For, freed from the oppression of the Combination Acts in 1824, trade unionism fell into a trap of its own making.

In the early stages of the Industrial Revolution the movement was not only a response to exploitation: it was also a reaction to the working population's exclusion from the vote. By the same token the Combination Acts, and the other repressive measures which had gone before, such as the suspension of the Habeas Corpus Act, were the ruling class's reaction not to an economic but to a political threat, that of revolution at a time when the French war was being financed out of taxes which bore down heavily on the new landless industrial proletariat formed by the enclosures.

The new race of manufacturers could use the Acts as a means of keeping down wages; but this new class was itself largely excluded from the vote. This convenient legislation was placed in their hands by a landed class which went in fear of the revolution preached by the radicals in the trade union movement. The Reform Act of 1832, however, enfranchised this same manufacturing class, but not the dispossessed work-people crowded in the fetid cellars and back-to-backs of the new manufacturing cities of the midlands and the north.

This disappointment in turn led the whole trade union movement off after another hare: the vote. In 1833 hopes centred upon the new Grand National Consolidated Trades Union. The *Pioneer*, a newspaper circulating among builders, envisaged an organization in which every trade was represented at town, district and national level, with 'The King of England' becoming 'President of the Trade Unions'. Within a year of its formation the Grand National had 80 000 members, including some women, although they were organized into separate lodges. One such was the Lodge of Ancient Virgins, who notwithstanding their name proved to be good scrappers in the street fights that followed the launch of a Grand National campaign for a ten-hour day.

But the union was unworkable. It was too big and, in attempting to represent too many trades, it in the end served none. Finance, organization, communications were not sufficiently developed, and in the winter of 1834 it was dissolved. From then until the end of the 1840s, working people turned to Chartism. This movement, launched by Radical members of Parliament, revolved around a People's Charter of Six Points drafted in the form of a Parliamentary Bill, published in 1837. Among the points were the ten-hour day and the vote for all adults.

Reasonable though this might seem, as viewed from our times, the campaign increased the fears aroused by the Grand National among the ruling class. One reason was that the Charter coincided with a great slump in the manufacturing industry. Within five years, one in eleven people in some industrial districts was pauperized. The Grand National had been infiltrated by incendiaries, machine-smashers and mob orators; Chartism was even more frightening. Huge gatherings known as 'monster meetings' were held on the windswept moors outside the idle mill towns. Opponents of any change seized upon the rhetoric of the more virulent orators, and once more the democratic and peaceable combination of working people was held to be both revolutionary and treasonable.

In its later stages, indeed, it was linked by the newspapers and by politicians with the armed insurrections that took place throughout Europe in 1848. But by this time Chartism had collapsed without achieving any of its aims. It was to be more than twenty years before the energies dissipated on Chartism would again be harnessed in the cause of trade unionism, even among men. But for women, the situation was even worse. They had taken part in the Chartist marches and meetings, and many women's names are to be seen on the petitions and appeals presented to Parliament. Yet, by mid-century, women were finally established in the minds of employers as a useful reservoir of labour, when male labour was either scarce or restive in the pursuit of better pay and conditions.

To male trade unionists, especially those in skilled trades

threatened by mechanization, women workers were cheap labour and therefore a threat to living standards. Such unions as existed were usually craft unions; they had grown up in days before the revolution when a woman's job was either at home or in the fields. These unions had managed to keep an intermittent existence under repression only by secrecy and exclusiveness. And although the legal restraints were eased, they were replaced by the threat from machines that could be operated by unskilled women as well as by skilled men.

In these circumstances, after the big let-down of the Grand National, the failure of Chartism and the exclusion from craft unions, women were unable to develop a sufficiently vital trade union background to take them into the second half of the century. Thus began a tradition that is with us yet, although there are now signs, in the second half of this century, that both women and male trade unionists are beginning to sense this failure and to do something to put it right.

About the middle of the last century, however, the textile unions began to find a different answer to the problem of female workers. Many unions, including some in this industry, had sought an answer in exclusion or discouragement. The Potters' Union, for example, gave this warning to women about to start work on a new machine:

To maidens, wives and mothers, we say that machinery is your deadliest enemy, of all the sufferers by mechanical improvements you will be the worst. It is a systemised process to slow murder for you. It will destroy your natural claim to homes and domestic duties, and will immure you and your toiling little ones in overheated and dirty shops, there to weep and toil and pine and die.

However, a new spirit began to breathe through the movement in the middle years of the century, although it was to be another twenty years or so before there were any appreciable benefits for women. Trade unionists began to realize that the violence of the strike, the picket and the riot could not win against the violence of pay cuts, deductions, payment in kind from company stores, and dreadful conditions. In the last resort, the employer's violence was superior in strength, in money and in staying power. The boss had at his back the forces of starvation, prison and the soldiery.

But as the structure of business changed, so trade unionists changed with it. The factories, the mills, and the pits had begun as small businesses run by one man or controlled by one family. With the appearance of the joint stock company, however, this began to change. First, small businesses began to merge in the interests of reducing competition. There arose a new class living in whole or in part on the income from investment in such companies. Side by side with these, there arose a class of managers to look after these businesses but, unlike the founding entrepreneur, these men might have neither control nor a financial stake in the business beyond salary.

It began to dawn upon those still active in what remained of trade unionism after the collapse of Chartism that they must alter not only their aims but their methods if they, like the new shareholders, were to get their slice of the mid-Victorian cake. Unions began to reorganize nationally on craft lines, often throughout an entire industry. This clear break with the vague, amorphous structure of the Grand National permitted the formation of coherent financial units able to support paid officials – like the capitalists' hired managers. The officials were then set to haggling with the managers, with the strike not as a first but as a last resort. The new Model Unions, as they were known, had an intense regard for detail, rules and organization, all the better with which to give the lie to the old revolutionary smear. It is from this period that there dates the verbose, plodding committee man who is the despair of prime ministers and the butt of newspaper cartoonists. However, it was still not a world in which women were unreservedly welcome. Only in areas and in industries with considerable female representation were serious efforts made to recruit women.

The Lancashire cotton unions provided one example. In this industry, there were district lists of pay, based on piece-work rates, which did not differentiate between men and women. Men and women thus enrolled with the same contributions and benefits, including the right of election to union posts. By 1896 women formed half the union membership. However, it was only with the formation of the 'new' or general labour unions towards the end of the century that great willingness was shown to admit women to membership. In the 1880s, for instance, societies such as the Dock, Wharf and Riverside and General Labourers' Union took women into membership, as did many others.

It would be wrong, however, to assume that the development of women's trade unionism, such as it is, is the mere record of women's passive acceptance of what was handed down by their male colleagues. Women continued to be active leaders and members of the trade union movement but their efforts were directed into 'separate development', in the end a futile and costly adventure.

As we have seen, women were active in the trade union movement among the textile industries of the north and midlands in the first half of the last century. These were, however, regions with unusual traditions of solidarity among working people, regardless of sex. Elsewhere, the pattern was for women to organize into separate unions, usually smaller, worse organized, and weaker than those of the men. Between 1825, when trade union association became legal, and the outbreak in 1914 of the First World War, the movement evolved first into a lawful, then a powerful and a durable force. During that war it was in consultation with the trade unions that the government framed its plans for placing British industry on a war footing.

The women's movement missed the middle phase of

consolidation and passed straight from the missionary to the establishment phase. This they did by merging into the men's organizations as soon as opinion in the men's movement had sufficiently softened to the idea. But it was not until the formation of general labour unions in the last quarter of the nineteenth century that women were welcome on a large scale in the male labour movement.

The effect of this was to exclude many women from the skilled trades, just as the new professional associations were to exclude women from the professions. Yet even had more unions taken women into membership from the start, women workers would still have been difficult to organize effectively. The jobs that most women did were so poorly paid that many either could not or would not pay union dues. In any case, the largest element in the female work-force – domestic servants – were liable to victimization or dismissal for joining a union. And when educated women began to move into clerical jobs they, like their male colleagues, at first identified themselves with the boss, and considered union membership beneath them.

Finally, marriage put an end to steady work for the majority of women, who accordingly considered their working lives too short for a union to achieve much on their behalf. Until past mid-century therefore, the mainstream union movement was content to limit its interest in women's employment to the issue of preventing women workers from competing with men. There were, however, rare spirits among both sexes who thought differently. It is due to their exertions in organization and publicity, and to those of women workers in the war effort, that the male and female trade union movement at last coalesced in the 1920s.

Perhaps the first national figure in the women's trade union movement was Emma Paterson, who in 1874 founded a body that came to be known as the Women's Trade Union League. This was not so much a trade union as a protective movement, a loose alliance of well-heeled sympathizers. These, like the Liberal politician, Sir Charles Dilke, and his second wife, Lady Emilia, saw the trade union movement as the best way of maintaining and improving the wages and conditions of women workers. Their object was to persuade women to join or form unions, and where possible the League would raise the money to fund stoppages.

Mrs Paterson, was persuaded by what she had seen of women's unions in the United States to support two basic propositions by no means widely accepted in Britain at the time: first, that women were not unsexed by working, as some male trade unionists asserted; and, secondly, that low wages and bad conditions were not part of heaven's plan for making full-time housewifery more attractive but a convenient device for cutting costs, first of female, and, by extension, of male labour. While in America she was impressed by what she saw of the operations of two women's unions in New York, the Parasol and Umbrella Makers' Society and the Women's Typographical Society. Mrs Paterson and her supporters helped to form and to sustain a number of women's trade unions in this country, of which only two lasted any length of time.

These were the Society of Upholsterers and the Society of Women Employed in Bookbinding, which became prominent in 1874. Mrs Paterson herself was one of the first women delegates to the Trades Union Congress, and from 1875 until her death eleven years later, at the age of thirty-eight, she sought to express women's grievances.

Henry Broadhurst, secretary of the Parliamentary Committee (later the General Council), opposed the presence of Mrs Paterson and her supporters, partly because he did not consider them *bona fide* workers, and partly because he 'doubted the wisdom of sending women to these congresses, because under the influence of emotion they might vote for things they would regret in cooler moments'.[2]

Incidentally, Broadhurst, once an Oxfordshire stonemason, became the first working man to become a Minister, when

Gladstone made him Under-Secretary at the Home Office in 1886. Thirty-seven years later, Margaret Bondfield became the first woman Chairman of the General Council, and she also became the first woman Minister, Parliamentary Secretary to the Ministry of Labour.

In 1874 Congress had resolved to 'promote the self-relying Trade Union movement among women'. Three years later, it was arguing that 'the duty of men and husbands is to bring about a condition of things when their wives should be in their proper sphere of home instead of being dragged into competition of livelihood with the great and strong men of the world'. In 1884, the Nut and Bolt Makers, alarmed at the organizing activities of the league among women, was asking Congress to 'stamp out the iniquitous system of female labour'.[3] The Nail Makers, on the other hand, were asking Parliament to restrict women workers to the manufacture of 'their own size of nail'.[4] But these were the last gasps of active hostility towards women workers. In 1885, after ten years' attendance by Mrs Paterson and her supporters Congress resolved that 'where women do the same work as men they shall receive equal pay'.

From this time onwards, the bigger general unions began to admit women. In 1889 the League supported a strike of girls employed in the East End works of the matchmakers Bryant & May. In that year the Fabian essayist Annie Besant had written an article describing the plight of these girls. They were badly paid and exposed to phosphorus poisoning, which caused great pain and caused the teeth to drop out. Emboldened by the article, the girls came out. In response, Bryant & May at first threatened to import blacklegs from Glasgow and then to remove the factory to Norway.

The Times, its arteries hardening after the great libertarian struggles of the first half of the century, was moved, perhaps by the fact that one of the organizers was the daughter of Karl Marx, Eleanor Aveling, to pronounce the strike to be the result not of incompetent, grasping management but of 'the class war which the body of socialists have brough into being'.

But the girls won. Negotiations with the management wer carried out on their behalf by the London Trades Counci formed by the League seven years earlier to promote contac between the women's unions in the capital. The Leagu itself raised £400 to enable the girls to stay out while talk went on. In a gesture unusual among political theorists Annie Besant followed up her article by becoming secretar of a new Union of Women Matchmakers. But effectiv though the League could be in selected disputes and in countering trade union opposition to women, the centur closed with few women in trade unions. In their *History o Trade Unionism* Sidney and Beatrice Webb estimated tha in 1891 less than one in 200 women manual workers was in union, compared with one in five men.

The League invited the big general unions to affiliate with it at a fee of a halfpenny a year per women member, in return for which it offered the services of a woman organizer The work of organizing women was carried on into the new century by an offshoot of the League, the National Federa tion of Women Workers, led by the secretary of the League Mary Macarthur. By this time, women workers who had previously stood aloof from trade unionism were beginning to organize. Among them were the clerks, the shop assistant and the warehouse workers. The federation was founded on the model of the new general unions and affiliated to the TUC.

Miss Macarthur, like Mrs Besant before her, was an indefatigable publicist. She secured the help of the edito of the *Daily News*, A. G. Gardiner, in a campaign to expos the conditions under which women were working in the sweated trades of clothing in London, and chainmaking in Birmingham. In 1906 the *News* staged an Exhibition o Sweated Trades at Queen's Hall, London. The result was to bring home to an affluent middle-class public the suffering upon which their comfort was based. An Anti-Sweating League sprang up in the same year, led by J. J. Mallon. Its aims were the creation of a system of trade boards (now known as wages councils) of employers, employees and government representatives. These would have the power to fix legally enforceable minimum rates in industries where union organization was too weak for effective collective bargaining.

The first object was to enlist the support of the men's trade unions, which was achieved at a conference in the Guildhall that same year. Before long, a Select Committee of the House of Commons was investigating this industrial abuse. Miss Macarthur, a most persuasive speaker, gave evidence which won over some hostile MPs. And in 1909 a Trade Boards Act was duly passed.

5. The professions close ranks

He considered that women had already established their competence in the professional engineering field. What he was really not satisfied about at the moment was the appropriateness of women in a professional capacity.

Personnel Director

Women workers, as we have seen, were excluded from opportunities in many mushrooming industries by the attitudes of male trade unionists. In the professions too, women were losing ground that they had long held. In the eighteenth century there were many women auctioneers, booksellers and printers. In what then passed for the medical sciences there were many women oculists, dentists and surgeons. *The Compleat Serving Maid*, a book of 1700, warned that all housekeepers should have 'a competent knowledge in Physick and Chyrurgery, that they may be able to help their mained, sick and indigent Neighbours: for commonly, all good and charitable ladies make this a part of their Housekeepers business'.

At that stage of medical knowledge, there may have been little to choose between the doctor and the housekeeper; if anything the housekeeper might have been the safer bet, since she would be more likely to give careful nursing. In 1739, we find Parliament granting £5000 to a Mrs Joanna Stephens on conditions he makes known for public use 'her Method of preparing her Medecines'. Many such women were widows or daughters carrying on the family business after the male practitioner had died.

As working men banded into trade unions, so those in the professions began to form themselves into associations. The Royal College of Surgeons was founded in 1800. Fifteen years later, the Society of Apothecaries was enabled by a Bill of Parliament to examine all apothecaries in England and Wales. The society required five years' apprenticeship, which included 'walking the hospitals' before examination. The hospitals themselves began to organize their own medical schools, which soon supplanted the apprenticeship system and encouraged specialization. Dentistry, too, was leaving behind tooth-drawing origins and was growing into a profession.

The motives of the members of these professional associations were different from those of the working men in the trade unions, although in excluding women the effects were the same. The professionals were better paid and felt less threatened by the changes taking place in society. However, as the eighteenth century gave way to the nineteenth there were only three professions outside the service of the Crown that offered both a career and a good social standing. These were medicine, law and the Church.

In medicine, where women were well established, the impetus to reform was especially strong. The pressure came not from above but from below. The Royal College of Physicians, founded in the seventeenth century, was recruited mostly from Oxford and Cambridge and had done little for medical education. Surgeons, conscious of their origins in the barber's shop, and apothecaries, who still ranked as tradesmen, supported the establishment of the Royal College of Surgeons. Like the guildsmen of previous centuries, they considered that the way to raise standards was to restrict entry.

This was accomplished, in the case of the doctors, by registering only those practitioners who had passed examinations set by the profession itself. Under the Medical Act of 1858 doctors had to be registered with a medical council and to show documentary evidence of their qualifications. Not until 1877, however, would any examining body allow women to qualify, even when they had completed exactly the same courses. In that year the Royal Free Hospital, London, agreed to admit women to its medical school, and the Irish College of Physicians agreed to act as examiner.

As with the unions, this only came about after a campaign by women reformers. These had to contend not only with the self-interest of male practitioners concerned to improve the standards and the repute of their calling but also the Victorian belief that women of a certain station should not work.

Indeed, such was the squalor of the hospitals of the time that only women of the lowest orders were thought fit to be subjected to the sights, sounds and smells to be found there. Dickens' drink-sodden nurse, Mrs Gamp, repulsive as she is, represents only a bowdlerized version of the real thing.

In 1854 the head nurse of a London hospital told Florence Nightingale:

In the course of her large experience she had never known a nurse who was not drunken, and there was immoral conduct practised in the very wards, of which she gave me some awful examples. . . . Nurses slept in the wards where they nursed, and it was not unknown for nurses of male wards to sleep in the wards with the men.[1]

In 1840 the prison reformer Elizabeth Fry helped to found an institute of nursing connected with Guy's Hospital, Southwark. But nursing was not to become a career for 'respectable' women until long after Florence Nightingale's exploits in the Crimea during the winter of 1854–5, and her subsequent foundation of a nursing school at St Thomas's Hospital, Lambeth.

Until the middle years of the century, however, contemporary notions of propriety and the exclusion of most women from secondary education prevented a new generation of qualified female practitioners from taking the place of the lady quacks of half a century before. In 1856 women offering themselves as candidates for a medical diploma at London University were refused by this, an institution founded by the libertarian reformers of the 1830s. For by now the exclusion of women had become an article of faith. By 1859 one solitary woman had slipped through the net. This was Elizabeth Blackwell, who succeeded in registering on the strength of medical qualifications obtained in the United States ten years before.

Within a year, the profession had acted to stop the loophole. A new charter was secured which excluded all holders of foreign degrees. In reply Miss Blackwell gave a series of lectures in London on the suitability of the medical profession for women. One of the listeners at her first lecture was a Miss Elizabeth Garrett, who not only decided to become a doctor, but had the support of her father. In 1860 she became a nurse at the Middlesex Hospital and thus began to attend medical lectures. But when she won higher marks than the male students admittance to further lectures was denied her. Miss Garrett persevered, and in 1865 managed to be registered by the Society of Apothecaries, having discovered that the charter of that body did not permit her exclusion. She later took a medical degree in Paris, but by 1870 she and Miss Blackwell were still the only two female medical practitioners in Britain, and both had qualified overseas.

The breakthrough did not take place till seven years later, with the case of Sophia Jex-Blake. Having qualified in Berne, Miss Jex-Blake successfully re-presented herself for examination at Dublin. But her success came only after a decade of struggle against the entrenched self-interest and misogyny of the medical profession. She had begun at Edinburgh in 1869 where she tried to attend lectures, but was forced to admit defeat after a long legal wrangle instituted by her fellow students. In the interval, Miss Jex-Blake had been joined in Edinburgh by four other women, and she hired a lecturer to teach them.

One of the girls, Edith Peachey, came third to two second-year men in an examination when only in her first year. The first three places carried with them the right to free use of the university laboratories. But the scholarship which was by right Miss Peachey's was offered to the man who came below her in the pass list. In 1872, at the time of the graduation examinations, the university denied that it had any power to give degrees to successful women candidates, but would award a 'certificate of proficiency', which would not entitle the holder to practise. Miss Jex-Blake took the university to court and lost. In the meantime, she failed her examinations, as did many male students that year who had not faced the same wall of obstruction and victimization. She and her companions dispersed, some like Miss Jex-Blake to foreign universities, and some to matrimony.

But first Miss Jex-Blake continued the battle in London. she agitated for Parliamentary action to confer upon unwilling universities the power to admit women, and to recognize the validity of foreign degrees. Meanwhile, she and Miss Garrett took a house in Hunter Street (later to become the London School of Medicine) converted it into a medical school, and tried every means of attaining official recognition. At one moment they seemed to have succeeded, by joining the Midwifery Board. This, they discovered, had the same legal standing as the Royal College of Surgeons, in so far as it could issue a licence permitting the name of its holder to be enrolled on the medical register.

But when they tried to use the licence in this way, the entire board of examiners resigned and the board was wound up. In the same year of 1875, however, the Bill enabling the universities to confer degrees upon women was passed. Within two years of the passing of the act, Miss Jex-Blake had qualified at Berne and been passed at Dublin. The log jam had been broken.

Education was, as Miss Jex-Blake found, the key to the now tightly organized professions. But although British universities could from 1875 choose to confer degrees upon women, Oxford refused to do so until 1920 and Cambridge until 1947. The academics maintained that they were merely obeying the founders' wishes, since the colleges had been established when only boys were given a secondary education. However, as A. J. P. Taylor points out, 'They were themselves disregarding these wishes by marrying and by not taking a religious test.'[2]

Until well into the nineteenth century boys and girls alike were given a primary education of sorts in private schools, often run by a woman, open to the children of any parents who could afford the fees of a few pence a week. At the secondary level, however, things were very different. Not until 1880 was education compulsory for either sex, and then only between the ages of five and twelve, while school fees were not abolished until 1891. Not until after the First World War were the education committees of local authorities obliged to provide education above primary level. Even then, eight out of ten children went straight to work on reaching the leaving age of fourteen.

Thus many boys, as well as girls, were denied a secondary education. But in addition the daughters of many comfortably-off and even rich families were excluded from the education offered their brothers. Until well into the last century secondary and further education were provided by the endowed schools and by the older universities, principally Oxford and Cambridge. These 'had been founded to ensure a sufficient supply of "fit persons to serve God in Church and State", and it rarely seems to have occurred to pious founders that women could be included in that category'.[3]

The endowed schools were founded with money or 'endowments' provided by merchants, noblemen, guilds or a

City livery company. One, Lady Manners' School, Bakewell, was endowed by a woman, but this was an exception. Winchester, founded in 1382 by William of Wykeham, sent its boys on to New College, Oxford. Eton, founded in 1440 by Henry VI, was linked with King's College, Cambridge. Girls on the other hand, were usually educated at genteel little private schools or at home by a governess, and the object of the education was marriage.

Marriage, as we have seen, was for much of the nineteenth century almost the only career open to a middle-class woman. Daughters of respectable though poor families could without stigma become governesses, but while this was socially acceptable it had few other advantages. A governess's main task was to prepare her female charges for marriage – the situation which had eluded her.

Whether taught at home or in a private school a girl was supposed to learn the 'accomplishments' which made a woman attractive to her future husband and might occupy her mind during her future idleness, rather than the skills which might equip her for a career in the new professions. Such airs and graces were considered enough to catch a husband, while conventional morality was sufficient to hold him. In her poem *Aurora Leigh*, Elizabeth Barret Browning describes the kind of education to be had from a governess of the time.

> I learnt the royal genealogies
> Of Oviedo, the internal laws
> Of the Burmese empire – by now many feet
> Mount Chimborazo outsoars Teneriffe,
> What navigable river joins itself
> To Lara, and what census of the year five
> Was taken at Klagenfurt – because she liked
> A general insight into useful facts. . . .
> I danced the polka and Cellarius,
> Spun glass, stuffed birds, and modelled flowers in wax,
> Because she liked accomplishments in girls.

The system was not universally accepted. In 1810, for example, Sydney Smith asked:

Why the disproportion in knowledge between the two sexes should be so great, when the inequality in natural talents is so small; or why the understanding of women should be lavished upon trifles, when nature has made it capable of higher and better things.[4]

Smith condemned the emphasis on drawing, music and dancing on the grounds that these aimed 'only at embellishing a few years of life, which are themselves so full of grace and happiness, that they hardly want it; and then leaves the rest of existence a miserable prey to idle insignificance'.

He contrasted the current tendency with that of a century before when the taste was for housewifery, and advocated an improvement in the education of women, 'to give to children resources that will endure as long as life endures'. But Smith appeared to accept the proposition that women would have little to do outside the home.

Their exemption from all the necessary business of life is one of the most powerful motives for the improvement of education in women. Lawyers and physicians have in their professions a constant motive to exertion; if you neglect their education, they must in a certain degree educate themselves by their commerce with the world . . . [Women] have nothing to do; and if they come untaught from the schools of education, they will never be instructed in the school of events.

One consequence of the prevailing attitudes towards women's education was a serious over-supply of governesses. Not only were too many girls forced into the work through lack of other opportunities, but not a few were unfitted by their own education to face competition from Swiss and French governesses, many of whom could boast some form of paper qualification. A mock advertisement printed in a contemporary issue of *Punch* illustrates their condition.

Wanted, a young lady who has had advantages, for a situation as governess. To sleep in a room with three beds, for herself, four children, and a maid. To give the children their baths, dress them and be ready for breakfast at a quarter to eight. School 9–12 and half past 2–4, with two hours' music lessons in addition. To spend the evenings in doing needlework for her mistress. To have the baby on her knee while teaching, and to put all the children to bed. Salary £10 a year and to pay her own washing.

The unfavourable position of governesses was an important factor in the movement to make a solid secondary education available to more women. The philosopher Frederick Denison Maurice became interested in the situation through his sister, Mary, who was a governess. He and other friendly academics decided that the best course was to improve women as teachers so that they might command better pay. In 1848 Maurice and his friends set up Queen's College, London, and in 1849 Mrs Reid founded Bedford College. These were modelled on King's and University College, London. Women of all ages flocked to the two colleges. At first the tuition given was simple enough: elementary grammar and arithmetic. Soon, however, advanced lectures on science, sociology and literature were also being provided and eagerly attended. George Eliot was a pupil at Bedford College, and at Queen's Sophia Jex-Blake was first a pupil and then a lecturer in mathematics.

Also at Queen's were two pioneers of secondary and further education for women: Frances Buss (1827–95) and Dorothea Beale (1831–96). Miss Beale went from Queen's to teach at the Clergy Daughters' School at Cowan Bridge which Charlotte Brontë, a former pupil, used as the basis for Lowood in *Jane Eyre*. In 1858 she was appointed headmistress of Cheltenham Ladies' College, founded five years earlier and modelled on the local boys' college. Miss Beale fought the shortage of trained teachers and the hostility of parents to develop a school of high quality. She also opened

St Hilda's College, which began as a hall of residence for
Cheltenham girls who wanted to go on to Oxford.

Miss Buss began as a teacher in a private school run by
her mother. After finishing at Queen's she returned to take
over the school, now known as the North London Collegiate
School. In 1871 she made over her property in the school,
thus establishing it as a 'public' school in the English sense
of the word, similar to the endowed schools for boys. By
this time, the North London had become a model for a
number of private ventures, notably the Girls' Public Day
School Trust, whose patron was Princess Louise, fourth
daughter of Queen Victoria. This organization had opened
its first school in 1873 in Chelsea, and within twenty years the
Trust was operating thirty-six schools up and down the
country.

Miss Buss and Miss Beale were given the opportunity to
express their views in evidence to the Schools Inquiry
Commission, known as the Taunton Commission, which was
established in 1864 to investigate the state of middle-class
education, other than in the great public schools. Its report,
published in 1868, focused national attention on the generally
deplorable condition of women's secondary education.
Taunton's Commissioners had been nagged into investigating female education, and as well as taking evidence from
reformers it examined girls' schools in several districts. This
proved particularly useful, since the fact that girls' schools
were private prevented much being known about conditions
there.

It cannot be denied [said the report] that the picture brought
before us of the state of Middle-Class Female Education is, on
the whole unfavourable. The general deficiency in girls' education
is stated with the utmost confidence, and with entire agreement,
with whatever difference of words, by many witnesses of authority.
Want of thoroughness and foundation; want of system; slovenli-
ness and showy superficiality, inattention to rudiments; undue
time given to accomplishments, and those not taught intelligently

or in any scientific manner; want of organisation – these may sufficiently indicate the character of complaints we have received in their most general aspect.

The blame lay largely with parents who, like Mme de Genlis, thought that 'girls are less capable of mental cultivation, and less in need of it, than boys; that accomplishments, and what is showy and superficially attractive, are what is really essential for them; and in particular, that as regards their relations with the other sex and the probabilities of marriage, more solid attainments are actually disadvantageous rather than the reverse'.

The Commissioners called for publicly managed day schools for girls, charging only moderate fees, in any town 'worthy of a grammar school'. There should also be further education for women. A year later the Gladstone government passed an Endowed Schools Act, containing the proposal that 'provision should be made as far as conveniently may be for extending to girls the benefits of endowments'.

Where the endowments of schools were not fully employed in educating boys, therefore, the extra cash was used to start new schools for girls or to revive old ones. One of the first was at Bradford, and soon there were others at Bedford, Birmingham and elsewhere. One of the boys' schools affected was Christ's Hospital, founded at about the same time as Eton for the benefit of both sexes. When investigated by the Commissioners in 1865 it was found to be educating 1224 boys to 22 girls. Even today fewer girls than boys benefit.

The spread of secondary education, first to the daughters of parents who could afford to pay for it and then to those who could not, came too late to assist women's entry into the newer professions. There were a range of callings, such as accountancy and company secretaryship, which came into existence in the last quarter of the century as a result of changes in business and commercial life. With the institution of the limited liability company, issuing shares to the public, control of business passed from the hands of the owner-entrepreneur to a board of directors acting on behalf of the shareholders. Thus, as R. C. K. Ensor writes, 'for the alert individual carrying his business in his head came to be substituted a collectivity finding safety in rules and records'.[5]

The Institute of Chartered Accountants in England and Wales was incorporated in 1880, and the Society of Incorporated Accountants was established five years later. These new professions, like medicine and the law, also sought to exclude women.

In 1889 the issue of women's admission was brought before the S.I.A. annual general meeting, and rejected by 229 votes to 88. Women were not in fact admitted until after the First World War. Incidentally, the first woman to pass the final exams and become an associate (1920) was the daughter of the association's president. The first woman articled clerk to qualify (1922) had been articled to her father. According to the society's history, a leading member was recorded as saying:

Accountancy was amongst those professions which required for their proper fulfilment those masculine qualities and experience of the world and intellectual capacity and courage which were very rarely to be found in members of the weaker sex.[6]

Although the new professions were anxious to imitate their more illustrious colleagues in medicine and the law, the basis of their anti-feminism was the business philosophy of the small firms from whence they sprang. Dickens' *Dombey and Son*, which first appeared in monthly instalments between 1846 and 1848, provides an insight into this thinking.

Dombey is a merchant whose business is carried on 'within the liberties of the City of London', near the Bank of England. But he and the family do not live above the shop, as his father might have done, but in 'a tall, dark, dreadfully genteel street in the region between Portland Place and

Bryanston Square'. Fanny Dombey's only contribution is to do the honours at home and to provide Mr Dombey (and the business) with an heir. Hitherto, however, she has been able only to produce a daughter. 'In the capital of the House's name and dignity, such a child was merely a piece of base coin that couldn't be invested – a bad Boy – nothing more.'

Here we see a classic example of the divorce between home and the place of work, and the relegation of the woman of affluent circumstances to sexual object, breeder, and chattel.

Although they refused to allow women into their ranks, the new professions found that they needed large numbers of them in subsidiary roles. Similarly, the doctors were inflexibly refusing women the right to qualify, but their brand new teaching hospitals could not function without a well-trained and educated corps of female nurses. In business, the flood of paperwork let loose by the new need for accountability soon overwhelmed the number of literate men available to handle it.

It was the Civil Service which showed the way. As a result of the Telegraph Act of 1869, the inland telegraph was nationalized under the Post Office. The Postmaster General was obliged by the Act to take over the staff as well as the equipment of the private companies, and discovered to his consternation that about a dozen women were employed as telegraph operators. By the standards of the time it was immoral for the sexes even to meet in a place of business. In 1870 we find this unhappy man describing his employment of women as 'a hazardous experiment'. Two years later, he is announcing 'with pleasure' that more women are to be taken on. When jobs for twelve junior counter-women were advertised, over 1200 women applied

On the whole [one official reported] it may be stated without fear of contradiction that if we place an equal number of females and males on the same ascending scale of pay, the aggregate pay to

he females will always be less than the aggregate pay to the males;
hat within a certain range, duty will be better done by the females
han the males, because the females will be drawn from a some-
what superior class; and further, that there will always be fewer
emales than males on the pension list.

Lack of other employment opportunities, he added, meant
hat wages (which would only attract men from an inferior
class) would pull in women from a superior class, who
moreover were less likely to combine in pursuit of higher
wages. Lastly, in one swoop conventional morality was
ssuaged and the pension list kept small by obliging female
ivil servants to resign on marriage, a practice that was
abandoned only in 1946.

The Civil Service thus showed the new professions a
olution to their problems of staff shortage. It demonstrated
hat this reserve of able female workers existed, and that it
was both more docile and cheaper than men. Moreover,
many a Victorian papa, whether running his own business or
umbered with unmarried daughters, could accept with
quanimity the prospect of his girls working for a living,
eeing that it was encouraged by no less an authority than
ne Civil Service, whose prestige had been greatly enhanced
y the reforms of 1870.

The need for such an accommodation became increasingly
cute as the century wore on. Between 1830 and 1875 five
million people emigrated from Britain. Most of these were
oung men, whose departure caused an imbalance in the
opulation of marriageable age. To this was added the barrier
class, for although many 'respectable' young men went
verseas, most women of their rank and age group stayed at
ome, despite the efforts of such bodies as the Female
Middle Class Emigration Society. Thus not only were there
ore marriageable women on the market, but also there
as less for them to do at home than there had been in the
edominantly rural society of the eighteenth century.

Domestic servants were as plentiful and as cheap as ever, and much of the food that had formerly been baked, preserved or brewed at home was now readily available from the new chains of grocery stores like Sainsburys (which by the 1890s had 200 shops in the London area alone). The first type-writers began to appear on the market in the 1870s, and although they were not in general use in Britain until the 1890s (significantly enough with the Civil Service) they eased the entry of women into offices. It was entry, how-ever, not into the new professions of accounting, office management and company secretaryship, but to routine office chores.

The arrival of large numbers of women in office work threatened the status of the men already employed there. Before mass education, the clerk was distinguished among other workers not so much by his earnings, as by his literacy and his practice of assuming the clothes and attitudes of his employer. His skills were in shorthand and book-keeping. But the coming of mass education devalued his literacy, and the arrival of the women drove down his pay. In part this was because there were so many women chasing each job. In part, both they and the male clerks were victims of the Victorian passion for gentility. Parents forced to let a girl work would sometimes have her typing by the sheet at home. Even if the girl went out to work, she was usually still living at home, in which case wages could be pitched accord-ingly. It was common for parents still to bear the cost of feeding and lodging their girl, with her earning only enough from working full-time to dress herself. This was the start of the pernicious doctrine that women should work only for pin-money.

Men were harmed by the wage competition, while un-supported women suffered in being paid the rates properly applicable to girls still partially supported by their parents

Accordingly, the men took steps to protect themselves Until the last war there were separate male and female

trade unions. As businesses became bigger and more specialized, the men took care to band into quasi-professional
groups limiting access to their jobs, as in the case of the
accountants, to men. Whereas overstocking had earlier
constantly blurred the distinction between the governess and
the domestic servants, the growing specialization of office
functions in turn served to debase clerical employment from
what it had been in mid-century, a way to managerial
status, and into another form of domestic service, although
this time its centre was the typing pool rather than the
kitchen.

6. The two world wars: votes and jobs

Some years ago I ventured to use the expression 'Let the women work out their own salvation.' Well, Sir, they have worked it out during this war.

Herbert Henry Asquith.

If, by the turn of the century, women were better organized in their work, it was still in work that was mostly boring, dirty and badly paid. Moreover, the new jobs opening up to them at the start of the present century could be done only in competition with men. Automatic machines, like the water or steam driven ones of a century before, served only to widen the gulf between men and women trade unionists. In Birmingham and in Coventry, it was said, 'there are many machine shops where the work is principally done by women and girls. They are, of course, got at a much lower rate of pay.' With the outbreak of war in 1914, however, the old antagonisms between men and women workers were put to one side. The war seemed for a while to produce many changes in the attitudes of both trade unionists and of politicians towards women as workers.

In August 1918, for example, with less than three months of the First World War to run, there was a strike of the men and the women working on the London buses. The bus crews were members of the National Transport Workers' Federation, and they were quarrelling with the bus companies over a proposal to give the wartime cost-of-living bonus to men but not women, even when they were doing the same job. The strikers were agitating for the government's Committee on Production not only to give the rise to the women, but to consider 'the question of the relation of the wages of men and women', or, in short, equal pay. In the event, the strikers got an inquiry into the question of equal pay as well as the bonus demanded for the women. That the inquiry came out in favour of equal pay, and that nothing was done about it, need not detain us here. It is enough to note that then, in the closing months of that terrible war, women workers seemed on the verge of a great achievement, the recognition of the part they had played in the work of war.

Today, the interruption by industrial action of transport, fuel and power services is as much a part of everyday living as the rain. But the 1918 dispute brought the question of equal pay forcefully to the attention of a government for the first time since the issue had entered national politics with the Trade Union Congress of 1885. The inquiry, known as the Atkin Committee of the War Cabinet, recommended equal pay where women were achieving equal results with men under piece-work, when replacing a man or where agreement had been reached by employers and trade unions on women doing the same or similar work on a time basis.

The strike involved men forgoing wages at a time of rising prices in support not of themselves, but of the women, who a few years before were seen as the enemy of the working man. The women, moreover, were members of a mixed union and were doing the same work as men. Before the war, the work could not have been offered, and in any case many male trade unionists believed that women should form their own unions.

The London bus dispute was part of a new phenomenon, the identification of mutual interests between male and female workers. Transport, like engineering, was one of the areas of 'men's work' invaded by women as the fighting wore on, when it became clear not only that the war was going to last beyond Christmas 1914, but that it was going to be fought as much in the armament factories as in the trenches. The number of women working in transport, for instance, multiplied more than fivefold. They were the women who took the place of men going to the front and who helped provide the extra services to enable workers to get between their homes and the factories.

More and more of these workers were themselves women. Between 1914 and July 1918, the number of women in employment rose by over 1·3 million to over 7 million. The number of women in industry rose by nearly a quarter to nearly 3 million, a change that was even more significant than it looked because, as well as the influx of newcomers to industry, there was also an actual decline in the numbers employed in the traditional women's jobs in the textile and clothing trades.

In the metal trades, for instance, previously a male bastion, the number of women workers trebled. Most were employed on work previously done by men. In shellmaking, the single most important wartime trade, women were employed on all operations. The war also confirmed a trend that had been under way when the fighting started. More and more women came into commerce and government as clerks and secretaries. The Civil Service alone took on 163 000. An early consequence of the outbreak of war was an increase in unemployment, particularly of women. Then as now, women formed about a third of the work-force. However, they were even more concentrated than now in the clothing industry and in domestic service. It was not until mid-1915 that industry began gearing itself to the demands of the armed forces for uniforms, foodstuffs and munitions.

'Industry was dislocated, employers shut down their factories in panic, leaving their workers to starve or to enlist', wrote Sylvia Pankhurst.[1] Women, however, could not enlist. Nor were the dependants of soldiers at that time paid a separation allowance. Food prices began to soar, and the realities of world war began to dawn on the poor sooner than upon the well-to-do. By September 1914, the employment of men had contracted by 8·4 per cent. For women in the female trades of cotton and peacetime clothing, the figure was 14 per cent.

It soon became clear, however, that the government could only hope to cope with the demand for munitions by the recruitment into the engineering industry of unskilled workers and of women. Men were leaving the industry to fight at precisely the moment that the demand for munitions was climbing. Their replacement was called 'dilution'. The way in which dilution was carried out was almost as important as the deed itself. The men of the engineering industry were among the élite of the trade union movement, skilled and clannish. They had seen how in the textile industry the advance first of machines and then of women workers had permitted the owners to cheapen men's labour. The Amalgamated Society of Engineers, for instance, delayed the enrolment of women until another war, until 1943. The engineers for whom, as for everybody else, sectional interest still reigned paramount, stood firm behind a wall of restrictive practices.

The government, for its part, could go some way to compelling dilution under powers conferred by the Defence of the Realm Act, and more powers could be taken. However, a victory gained at the expense of industrial strife might prove to be no victory at all. Lloyd George, the Minister of Munitions, eagerly grasped an initiative when it was offered him by the unions. They would, they said, agree to dilution, but on two conditions. First, that it was to be carried through voluntarily; second, that it should be under the unions' direction.

The Treasury Agreement, as it came to be known, was historic in two senses: it paved the way for the successful prosecution of the war effort without coercion; and it marked the acceptance by the government of trade unions as the legitimate voice of working people. Unfortunately, this milestone was reached on the backs of women workers. In return for their co-operation, the unions, notably the engineers, secured three concessions. These were, first, that 'traditional', i.e. restrictive, practices should be restored at the war's end; second, that profits should be restricted and, third, that the unions should participate in the committees organizing dilution. The Board of Trade then issued a proclamation asking women to register for work through local labour exchanges. Many answered the call, some through deepening poverty, others through patriotism.

As is so often the case, the nationalistic passions aroused by war sidetracked the energies of groups and individuals hitherto campaigning for social ends. In July 1915, Christabel Pankhurst, the militant suffragette leader, led a demonstration of women down Whitehall. Their slogan was 'We want to serve'. 800 000 women went into engineering, 500 000 into clerical work in private offices and 200 000 into government offices. About 250 000 worked on the land, and many went into the transport services, where they worked as conductors on buses and trams. Nearly 100 000 joined the auxiliary services of the three armed forces, while as many again became nurses. Many well-to-do women worked in canteens and welfare services. In industry, the government, the engineering employers and the trade unions were content with the deal they had arranged on the employment of women.

Women had less cause to be so. At the time of the Board of Trade's proclamation, there were still women wage-earners out of work. It was not clear how well the women volunteers were to be paid. Men replacing skilled male workers would be paid 'the usual rate of the district for that class of work'. As for women, Lloyd George would only say that those undertaking the work of men would be paid the same rate as men for piece-work. This was clearly an opening for employers to pay women at time rates, which could be pitched lower for women than for men. By the time the engineers had woken up to this one, which of course threatened the prospects of those men now away in the forces on their return, it was too late. The government undertook to see that male wage rates were not undercut by the Munitions Act, which did add a measure of protection to the provisions of the Treasury Agreement admitting women to men's jobs.

But the Minister of Munitions could declare any munitions factory a 'controlled establishment'. In such an establishment profits and wages might not be raised without his consent, and any infringement was punishable by a fine. The Act also restricted workers' movements from one employer to another in search of better pay or conditions. Employers eagerly sought to come within the Act for the power it gave them over their workers. Gradually a situation grew up in which large numbers of women were obliged to work long hours for lower pay than that of men. In Leeds, a sixteen-year-old girl armaments worker was hurt in her machine after a $25\frac{1}{2}$-hour shift. She had begun work at 6 a.m. on a Friday, and taken off two hours for meals that day, with half an hour for breakfast on Saturday, on which day her accident took place at 7.30 a.m. A magistrate dismissed her case, saying, 'The most important thing in the world today is that ammunition shall be made.'

Wages did not catch up with prices until 1917, although by dint of working long hours women could make up the difference. To a degree, the fortunes of many women workers depended upon the willingness of male trade unionists to fight for them. Membership of the National Federation of Women Workers rose to 60 000 in 1919 from 11 000 in 1914. The federation gained representation on government committees concerned with women workers.

It also negotiated on women's behalf with the bigger and more powerful male trade unions. Some, like the railwaymen and the bakers, co-operated. Others, like the spinners and the brassfounders, did not. Where there was co-operation, women's wages tended to rise, whether they were doing 'women's work', or substituting for men. Most women were denied this help, and suffered accordingly. The situation was particularly bad in the new sweated trades. Such were the needs of the armed forces that a race of contractors sprang up to supply clothes and equipment. Factories were extended and houses converted into workshops. Many worked twelve hours a day, seven days a week.

A mother supporting six children brought me her pay envelope. In four hours she could make six soldiers' bags and received 5½d. In Bethnal Green, a contractor convicted of paying less than the already low official rate was fined 10s. [50p] for the first case and 2s. [10p] for seven others.[2]

The creation of a munitions industry to meet the demands of the war was a great achievement by any standards. It was also an achievement that would have been impossible without the contribution of women, whether voluntary of otherwise.

Magnificent though the contribution was, it should be remembered to what end it was directed. The war was begun in stupidity and conducted in a general atmosphere of unconscionable waste, both of human and of material resources. Women were needed in such large numbers because, in terms of current military thinking, men were the cheapest and therefore most expendable battlefield commodity. Had there not been such a squandering of men at the front, there would have been no need for women (and, in the sweatshops, children) to work such long hours.

A hundred years before, it had been demonstrated by industrial radicals such as Robert Owen and Lord Shaftesbury that goods are more efficiently produced by a healthy work-force working in short shifts. However, at Elswick, for example, it was found that women munitions workers were putting in an 84-hour week, even though there were plenty of other women available to share the work. The employers preferred to work their machines for two shifts of twelve hours rather than for three of eight hours. The very nature of much of the work was dangerous without the added risks of carelessness induced by fatigue or over-exposure to noxious chemicals. The work involved handling explosives, heavy metal casings and highly combustible chemicals like phosphorus.

Women were particularly prized in the aeroplane industry, for their manual dexterity enabled them to fabricate the frail machines better and faster than many men. But the work was carried out in unsupervised conditions, and involved dangerous exposure to the poisonous 'dope' used in the varnishing process. At one London factory, protected by the Munitions Act, overtime was compulsory and paid at mere time rates. On each shift of thirty girls, six would take turns to go outside the workshop to recover from the fumes.

Feminist writers are sometimes fond of looking back to the First World War as the dawn of a new day for their sex. It certainly seemed so at the time. The Suffragists, for instance saw in the war a chance to pursue the vote by the peaceful demonstration of women's capacity to work with men for the war effort, rather than through their previous tactics of firing buildings and mobbing His Majesty's Ministers. There were gains. Women of every degree had shown to their own satisfaction how outmoded had become Victorian ideas of woman as a male possession, a mere perpetuator of the race.

They had also brought south from the mills the idea that women were just as capable as men of doing many types of work previously closed to them. Prices doubled during the war, but the wages of working women went up much more. Over 400 000 domestic servants were able to find work and independence outside another woman's parlour. And if a grateful country had not seen its way to giving women equal pay for equal work, it had at least acknowledged the justice of such a claim. And in 1919 women aged over thirty were given the vote, and qualified women were given the legal right to enter most professions. Women had been accepted into male unions in large numbers. The number of women unions rose from 350 000 before the war to nearly 660 000 at its height. But then came the peace.

In 1921 the National Federation of Women Workers was merged with the National Union of General and Municipal Workers. Margaret Bondfield became the union's chief woman officer. The Women's Trade Union League became in turn the Women Workers' Group of the TUC Parliamentary Committee, or General Council as it was now called, again with Margaret Bondfield as chairman. Two seats in the General Council were then as now reserved for women. Yet the integration of the men's and the women's trade union movements, so long delayed and so harmful to the interests of women workers, was to betray the hopes of its advocates.

By 1921 the proportion of women in employment was less than before the war. The percentage of women factory workers, for example was 32·3 in 1913 and 32·8 in 1938, a figure broadly representative of the proportion of women to men in the labour force as a whole. There was some slight redistribution within some industries. The proportion of women in some metalwork factories doubled from 8·8 per cent in 1913 to 16·4 per cent, but in no one industry did the gains made during the war remain. Put simply, the extra women workers downed tools and went back to their kitchens. A few former domestics kept their work in the factories. Many clerks and secretaries remained in commerce and government. Equal pay, though promised, was not delivered. Union membership slumped. Yet now the women's unions were gradually being absorbed by the bigger men's unions, with the result that once peace came, women's interests were more of a minority cause than ever. The war had, it is true, represented a break with the recent past in employment matters. But it was a break quickly and fairly unobtrusively mended.

Women had entered the war out of necessity or out of patriotism, but still handicapped by the old assumptions that women, if they worked at all, did a different set of jobs from the men. It was the State that sought dilution. Furthermore, male trade unionists exacted as the price of their acceptance of dilution the promise from government and employers that, come peace, the women would go (most did so, and willingly). Finally, the acceptance by employers of women is often a consequence of full employment. With peace came not only the usual post-war contraction of industry, but later a slump that caused mass unemployment. It was the experience of the slump rather than of the war that has effectively coloured the attitudes of men and women workers ever since. Yet things could not slip back into exactly the same place. Some women were kept in the offices to keep up with the extra paper work in the new era of government intervention created by the war. The war also ushered in a situation in industry whereby women could be brought back without too much disruption of production should engineering again face sudden heavy demand, as happened twenty years later.

The need to train women in the First World War vied with the natural desire of male trade unionists not to teach them the whole of any engineering process. Employers were keen to co-operate, since the division of a process into several different components each carried out by a different woman was doubly attractive. It not only cut down the amount of training required by the women, and the enforced absence from their work by the male instructors, but also made it easier to duck paying male rates because the newcomers were not doing precisely comparable work. The device would also be used for taking on unskilled male labour and that, together with new machines being developed, became a standard part of post-war engineering. It was a device that helped keep some women in work once peace came.

It was the action of women MPs which led to the resignation in May 1940 of the pro-appeasement government led by Neville Chamberlain.[3] Labour had decided against forcing a division for fear that the Conservatives would rally to Chamberlain's support. The women MPs forced Labour's hand. They had an all-party room of their own, itself a sign that after twenty-one years they were still not regarded as members of their respective parties rather than women. Here they met and made their historic decision.

In October of the same year Ernest Bevin became Minister of Labour and National Service and took his place in the war cabinet. Throughout the previous war, Bevin had been leader of the dockers' union and a founder-general secretary of the Transport and General Workers' Union. Women had entered the transport industry in large numbers in the First World War and generally had been well treated by male trade unionists. But Bevin was not the man to repeat the mistakes of the First World War.

Bevin's predecessor at the beginning of that war, as 'the voice of labour' was Arthur Henderson, who was made President of the Board of Education, not the first priority of an embattled nation. No trade union official was employed at the Ministry of Munitions, although from time to time Henderson would be called in to conciliate. Bevin, however, was at the centre of things, and well placed to put into effect the lessons of that previous mean and wasteful conflict.

This was just as well, for the task ahead was enormous. Bevin came to office at a time when the lessons of the previous war seemed to have been forgotten. War was declared on 3 September 1939, although a fight had been widely expected for more than a year before. Yet in that same month the pattern of unemployment began to repeat the experience of 1914. Employment dropped by 75 750 for men, and rose by 175 000 for women. There appeared to be no official plans for involving women in the event of a further large-scale war. The reason appeared to be that senior civil servants at the Ministry of Labour had no wish to be involved in the preparations for an eventuality which in the previous war had caused so much friction with the unions. Bevin's own experience of that time, however, convinced him that the present conflict could no more be successfully prosecuted without the large-scale involvement of women than could the last.

The effects of the lack of planning were soon felt as the phoney war gave way to the real thing. By the time of the Dunkirk evacuation, a ludicrous situation had developed at home whereby the unemployment figures for women were worsening with the collapse of peacetime luxury industries, while the few women in the munitions industry were commonly working 36-hour shifts on rush jobs. Not only was this bad for the people concerned: it was also bad for production. After a short spurt, production would slip back even below normal as a result of spoilt work and absenteeism through overwork. It also happened that workers would tend to take a day off during the week, coming in on Sunday to finish the job on double time.

In June 1940 Bevin had to issue an order limiting women's hours of work to sixty a week. Then, after a shaky start, the government got down to waging war on a less amateurish and wasteful basis than last time. An inter-departmental Manpower Requirements Committee was set up to apportion the division of hands as between the forces and the industries needed to sustain them. Even the Army was given manpower totals within which it would have to operate. When the Committee had finished totting up industry's needs, the sums astonished the government.

By the end of 1941, it claimed, the armed forces and the munitions industry would need $8\frac{1}{2}$ million people where at the outbreak of war there had hardly been 3 million. Such an increase could only be met by ordering the less essential industries to release manpower. The mines and the railways were exempt, but in the case of the distributive industry up to half its manpower was to be released for active service. Even the munitions industry would have to free up to a tenth of its manpower for the forces. If the country were not to seize up as a result, then women must be brought in to take the places of the men who had left to fight. 'The famine for men would breed a hunger for women', says the official history of the time.[4]

The number of women who would have to be brought into the labour force was estimated by the Committee at over $1\frac{1}{2}$ million, when the total female labour force had in 1939 been only about 5 million. Bevin had at first hoped that enough extra women could be persuaded to come forward voluntarily. Some did so, but not enough, and not quickly enough. By the end of January 1941, Bevin was saying, 'We have now reached the stage where . . . we shall call into service many women who in normal circumstances would not take employment.'

In March the government used its powers under defence regulations to issue an order requiring women as well as men to register with their local labour exchanges.

The object of this was to find out just how many women there were actually in work or willing to work if the opportunity presented itself. It would also enable the government to find out how many women were 'mobile', that is, un-encumbered with domestic responsibilities and therefore able to move to areas where there were labour shortages. In December this order was followed by the National Service (No. 2) Act, under which all single women between twenty and thirty were conscripted for National Service, whether in the armed forces, in auxiliary services (as with anti-aircraft units) or in industries specified by the government. This was a clear break with the voluntary system that had operated in the previous war. Conscription of women on this scale was not attempted by any other of the belligerents in the Second

World War. By the end of 1943 women between the ages of eighteen and fifty were being registered and being directed to war work if there was no compelling domestic reason to the contrary.

In general, the system was administered humanely, and was successful because it was carried out with the consent of the people. In June of that year, the number of women in the work-force reached 7 million, and the proportion of women to men had risen from a quarter at the beginning of the war to a third, roughly the figure we have today. In fact, activity rates are now higher than at the height of the war.

For the first time, there were also many married women at work. The government pioneered the use of nurseries, and schemes whereby two married women could 'share' the same job, each putting in a half shift. Throughout, the war in the workshops was fought in a more businesslike way than in the Great War. There was no longer the feeling that production came first, and people a long way second. Hours were shorter and more supervised, and concern for the welfare of workers gave rise to what we now know as the personnel manager. Indeed, in the early days of its formation women were very well represented in the ranks of the Institute of Personnel Management. Later, as welfare work for women developed into a personnel management function covering both male and female employees, and the status of the job rose accordingly, the men began to take over the jobs. Once again, as in the Great War, women were doing many jobs formerly closed to them or regarded as beyond their capacity. The play was roughly the same as last time, but with more competent direction. The proportion of women in the metal manufacture, engineering and motor industry rose from about a fifth to over a half.

In the First World War men transport workers had come out on strike in favour of equal pay for their women workmates; in the Second, it was the turn of the engineering workers. In the summer of 1940 agreement had been reached between male workers and management in the industry that where women were employed to do the same work as men they should after thirty-two weeks receive the man's rate for the job. As in the last war, there was widespread evasion of the spirit of the agreement. During 1943 a dispute involving both men and women broke out at the Hillington (Glasgow) works of Rolls-Royce over management evasion of the 1940 agreement. The dispute ended in a victory for the workers, with every machine named in the agreement and the pay determined, not by the sex of the operative, but by the work done on the machine.

The Hillington plant was in a sense a product of the previous war in that, although newly built, it was designed to be operated largely by unskilled workers and by women, and only by a minority of skilled men. It was this introduction of mass-production techniques that, earlier in the year, had at last persuaded the Amalgamated Engineering Union to admit women, something that had never been agreed even at the height of the 1914–18 War. However, outside union and plant agreements there was little progress in the way of establishing female work as a permanent feature of the nation's industrial life.

Once again, the experience of war was held to be relevant only to that particular conflict. And although there was less of a shakeout after the war, this was not because of policy but because it was neither economically necessary nor politically possible to permit a slump of the magnitude that followed the previous war. Far from advancing the cause of equal pay, it might be more true to say that the war pushed it back even further. The 1918 transport strike was followed by the appointment of the Atkin Committee of the War Cabinet, which recommended the adoption of equal pay. In the Second World War disputes such as the Hillington strike were followed by a Royal Commission on Equal Pay, but after three years' deliberations, the Commission, under Sir Cyril Asquith, reached no clear conclusions, noting merely that by and large men and women were not employed in the same jobs, and that there was little pressure from the unions for political action to bring about equal pay. Idealistic arguments based on individual justice were rejected because 'perfect justice for all individuals in respect of rewards is not compatible with an economic system based on free choice and changing techniques'. The Royal Commission was in effect only echoing the views of the Prime Minister, Winston Churchill who, although loud in his praise of women's war efforts, was unwilling to offer any more tangible appreciation.

In 1944, for example, he quashed a proposed amendment to the Education Act that would have given equal pay to women teachers, who were patently doing the same work as men. Thus, while the First World War had at least won women the vote, the Second World War, while making women's efforts compulsory rather than voluntary, offered no comparable benefit. Indeed, until well into the war, women at Government Training Centres were paid less than men, as were women suffering war injuries. Worse still, techniques developed out of a genuine desire to learn from the wasteful labour policies of the First World War began to be forgotten after the Second. Now in the 1970s, the idea of nurseries provided by the state or the employer, or the splitting of one full-time job between two married women working part-time, are still put forward as if these were novelties. The Government Training Centres opened to teach women men's jobs were twenty years later still only teaching men's jobs – to men.

7. Women's attitudes to work

Such discriminatory attitudes as are demonstrated by employers are not some peculiar viciousness of employers as employers but simply reflect the nature of a feature of British society which is, whether one likes it or not, discriminatory . . . a style of society that seems to be just as acceptable to very many women as it is to very many men.

Institute of Careers Officers

More women are consigned to low pay, routine work and poor prospects by their own choice than by the actions of misogynist employers.

The basic fact about the employment of women is that there are in reality two labour markets: one for men and one for women, with a very small overlap area between them . . . and it is well known that the customary women's jobs, with very few exceptions, are to be found at the bottom of the pile.[1]

Such a situation could never have developed, let alone persisted, without the acquiescence of many women. Nevertheless, legislation designed to 'eliminate discrimination between men and women in regard to pay and other terms and conditions of employment was not passed until 1970. This situation is related to a curious and comparatively recent view of what marriage is about. 'From being a financial bargain, an investment in social stability and a pact to perpetuate the line, it has largely become two people's attempt to perpetuate their love.'[2] Until the beginning of the last century this idea would have seemed absurd.

Even today, the cliché that a woman's place is in the home is believed by many men, and also by many women. Until the beginning of the last century, this was held to be self-evident. This was because for most people home was where much of the family's income or provisions were made. Until the 1880s, when universal education became available, it might also be where the children were educated.

Neither of these considerations is the case today. The work that women do, and always have done, to supplement the family income, has moved away from the home and into the office, the factory and the shop. In addition, the traditional products of woman's labour at home, the bread, the clothing, are now not made within the family but bought for it in shops from the money made in outside work. Marriage has brought with it economic duties, and with them the assurance of a certain economic status. Formerly, the economic and social status went together; they were not in conflict except at those times when pregnancy put an end to productive work in the home, and even then it was acknowledged that, in bringing children into the world, the mother was playing her part in seeing that both parents had some guarantee of protection when they should become old and weak.

However, as we have seen, a separation has occurred between the two parts of the dual function of women: as wife and mother, and as a contributor to the upkeep of the family. In the second role, most women once either contributed by making goods for sale outside, or reduced family expenditure by making clothes and growing or otherwise providing food.

Today, however, for better or for worse, many domestic activities – apart from straightforward housework – have been relegated to the status of pastime by the availability of highly competitive ready-made products on a more and more efficiently organized market.[3]

Women have been translated from producers into consumers even in these 'pastimes'. Home-baked bread, for instance, is likely to have been bought raw but ready-made in a pack. Now, when a family needs extra income, most women have to find employment away from the home. This is a clear break with the earlier tradition, where home was the focus of both roles. Parallel to the physical separation of these two roles there has grown up in the minds of men and women alike the fear that the economic role of woman is possibly inimical of her social role.

In the case of a married woman this may be expressed in a feeling of guilt that she should wish to continue working after marriage or when her children are at school. Others may feel that certain types of job or levels of responsibility are inherently unwomanly. Eleanor Macdonald has quoted the story of a firm that advertised for women to fill a job that paid £3500 a year. Not an application was received until the job was re-advertised at £1400. 'The girls,' Miss Macdonald says, 'just didn't have that grooming that a boy has, that gives him the conceit to make that leap from £1400 to £3500.'[4]

For many single girls work is seen as secondary and subordinate to the business of attracting a husband. There is an inability to recognize marriage as a state lasting many years and containing within its span many different phases. Too many girls, imbued with the notions of popular literature can see no further than the preliminary stages of marriage: courtship, the ceremony itself, the arrival of children.

But, of course, crowded and often happy though these years may be, they are not the whole story. In contrast to their grandmothers, most women now have their last child by the time they are thirty, and by the time they are thirty-five, the children are at school.

When a woman is having children she is at the centre of the stage, but then the children grow up and away from her. A frightful emptiness is bound to follow. . . . You have to have something else – to make you feel needed and wanted, and to make you feel that you're doing your stuff.[5]

As we have seen, women today live longer than before, have fewer children, and stop having them earlier. Thus, the amount of 'free' time available to a woman with children of school age is gradually lengthening. For too many women this time, which can already be twenty-five years or more, is spent working at some deadbeat job because they never trained for anything better before marriage. Nevertheless, many women seem resigned to the fundamental fact that industrial society, having taken women's work out of the home and into the factory and office, has yet to admit women to the new work-place on anything like terms of equality with men. A woman's place is still widely assumed to be in the home, although home no longer offers the same range of duties and satisfactions as in earlier times.

Thus, while women are quite willing to work, and indeed industrial society could not function if they were not, the job must be secondary to the social role of wife and mother. They are therefore required to confine themselves to a limited range of employments recognized as acceptable 'women's work'. These are usually the modern versions of jobs which were carried out in pre-industrial society by women in the home – nursing, teaching, food processing, spinning and weaving. However, the status of women in these employments is habitually regarded as secondary and supportive. Marriage is what counts, and the obsession with the marriage role of women, whether held by men or women, goes much deeper than the level of work responsibility at which it is thought proper for women to operate.

The obsession influences also the choice of career, and this is probably its most destructive manifestation.

It can be said that vocational influences become apparent even before the birth of a child in the fantasies that parents build around their offspring. . . . They may think that their daughters' careers do not matter as much as their sons'.[6]

In practice, this means that many parents see their daughters' future in terms of getting married and having children. Work, either before or after marriage, is seen as, at best, a means of financing the family or 'getting out of the home' for some company for a few hours a day.

This is an assumption passed on to the girls themselves from their earliest days, and constantly reinforced during childhood and adolescence by the media, the schools and employers themselves. Of parents' influence, Mrs M. Cooper, general secretary of the Institute of Careers Officers, has said, 'This is another argument for increasing our numbers from tomorrow morning, nine o'clock, because almost every survey done has shown adequately that the most influential group on young people's decision-making is that of the parents.'[7]

Unfortunately for girls and parents alike, this influence is often extremely inhibiting, since it is based on attitudes that are no longer appropriate. In 1965 a government social survey interviewed a national sample of 10 000 households on behalf of the then Ministry of Labour. The main purpose was to find out why women, and particularly married women, enter or do not enter employment.

In addition, however, the survey came up with many valuable pointers on women's attitudes to work in general. Fewer than 10 per cent of the women interviewed said that they were dissatisfied with their jobs. In fact, just over half said they were 'very satisfied'. Of these, the level of satisfaction was lowest among the sixteen to nineteen and twenty-five to twenty-nine age groups.

Very few women, about one in ten, were seriously thinking of changing their jobs. Nevertheless, the highest percentage of women thinking of changing was again among these two age groups. Audrey Hunt, the editor of the survey, said of the sixteen- to nineteen-year-olds that this group would include many girls who were in first jobs that had not lived up to their expectations. 'The older age group', she wrote, 'are of an age to assess the prospects of their jobs and it may be for this reason that the level of satisfaction was lower.'[8]

When it came to looking at workers according to their level of skill rather than their age, Ms Hunt found that semi-skilled manual workers were far less happy in their work than any other group. Indeed, the unskilled manual and personal service workers were among the most satisfied. 'Possibly those with little or no skills settle happily into undemanding jobs', she said, 'while those with more ability are dissatisfied with the limited opportunities open to them.'[9]

When Ms Hunt surveyed the reasons why married women returned to work, she found that over four-fifths of those interviewed said it was for the money. No other single attraction was named by even half that number. Ms Hunt's explanation for this is worth noting.

Undoubtedly, many working women were constrained to give an answer which they felt to be socially acceptable and therefore mentioned the reason for working which they considered would justify them in doing something not otherwise quite desirable.[10]

Since the earliest times, married women have been expected to work because of, not despite, their being married. As we have seen, male agricultural wages were for centuries calculated on the basis that a labourer's wife and family kept themselves. Nevertheless, we are now confronted with a situation in which marriage is still seen as the high point in a girl's life, and a career as somehow evidence of lack of commitment to that central role. This is widely felt not only by women themselves, but by male workmates, by trade unionists, by employers and by politicians. Sometimes this view is economically convenient in that it provides a justification for low pay.

On reaching school-leaving age 80 per cent of boys and 70–80 per cent of girls go straight into full-time work. But the figures suggest that girls irrationally tend to seek out jobs which offer them the least chance of continuing their general and vocational education, even though they are likely to be back at work within ten years of marriage. In 1971, for example, about 220 000 girls between the ages fifteen and seventeen left school to go to work, and about 242 000 boys. However, while 39·5 per cent of the boys went for jobs which, like engineering, offered apprenticeship to a skilled occupation, among girls the percentage was only 7·5. Of this group, about three-quarters went into hairdressing, where the apprentice system has been attacked as a method of providing cheap rather than trained labour.

The biggest identifiable single choice of work for girls was clerical employment, which attracted 35·8 per cent of the school-leavers, compared with 7·2 per cent for boys. Moreover, most clerical employers expect women to learn their shorthand and typing outside working hours. 'The fact that women themselves still appear willing to accept this situation is an indication of the change of attitudes still to be achieved.'[11]

Of the 220 000 girl school-leavers in 1971, 32 per cent entered the manufacturing and distribution industries. But although there are more women than men in distribution, employers are more than twice as likely to provide day-release education for a boy as for a girl. Nor is the situation better in manufacturing. Of sixteen sectors of manufacturing industry identified by the Department of Employment in 1969, three gave day-release to less than one in twenty of their girls. Nationally, one in ten girls get day-release, compared with about one in four boys. If one were to exclude national and local government employment, the figure for girls would drop by about a fifth.

Let us now return to hairdressing, since it is the choice of three-quarters of the girls who go into an occupation offering apprenticeship. But what does this apprenticeship mean?

You will find that in most hairdresser shops there are many apprentices and very few other workers because it is cheaper for employers to use apprentices as unskilled labour and they will be used mainly for things like washing hair and sweeping floors and they will get very little training indeed.[12]

In fact, though hairdressing is one of the most popular careers for girls, it is the one in which trade unions have the least power and governments the least interest. In 1972 two doctors, Professor C. N. Calnan and Dr Jean James, delivered a report to the Hairdressing Council on what they called 'the unnecessarily high risk of dermatitis to which apprentice hairdressers are at present exposed'. In a foreword to the report, two members of the Council wrote: 'Some apprentices carry out twenty or more shampoos a day and are also expected to clean out the salon. Is the performance of so many shampoos an essential part of training or does it represent a form of cheap labour?'

But these facts are unlikely to be generally known among the parents of girls interested in hairdressing as a career.

Since 1964, the industry has been under the eye of a statutory body, the Hairdressing Council – a development which trade unionists have sought for hairdressing since the turn of the century. However, the Council is a watchdog without teeth. Responsible in theory for the registration of hairdressers according to their training or qualifications the Council has succeeded, ten years after its foundation, in registering the names of only about 30 000 of the 120 000 people estimated to work in the industry.

In 1970, six years after the Hairdressing Council was established, the Industrial Training Service reported that the main problem facing the industry's training board was 'the lack of expertise of the majority of employers as regards methods of training, and appreciation of the value of training'.[13] The report continued: 'Although the current standards of internal training in the industry are very low, employers themselves are very satisfied with their present arrangements, and are unlikely to change unless there is a need to do so.'

In December 1969, a few months before it lost office, the Labour Government set up the Hairdressing and Allied Services Industry Training Board. But within eighteen months, the board was being wound up on the instructions of the new Conservative Secretary of State for Employment, Mr Robert Carr, on the grounds that more small employers needed exemption from the levy on payroll raised to finance industrial training boards. This had the effect of pulling out the financial rug from under the feet of the Hairdressing ITB, since over half the employers in hairdressing employed less than five workers. A few months later, the trade union delegation withdrew from the wages council that sets wages and conditions within the industry, 'because we could no longer be party to such low wage rates and inequitable wages structure'.

In this sort of situation, there is no bridge left between reality and the fantasies of girl school-leavers and their parents, who may honestly think they are doing their best for their daughters by encouraging them to enter an industry such as this.

Nor is collective bargaining able to remedy the obvious inequalities of the hairdressing industry, since wages are regulated by wages councils rather than by negotiations between management and trade unions. These councils are, as we have seen, composed of employers, trade unionists and officials of the DEP. In 1973, in the absence of trade union representatives from the wages council, the Secretary of State of the DEP made a new wages regulation order based upon an application from the council. According to this, after three years' 'employment as an apprentice' girls (and boys) could be paid £8·50 a week in London, and £8 outside. In addition, after two years' work as an operative hairdresser in a London ladies' salon a girl could be paid £14 a week, £1·45 less than a man. Even with the uncertain supplement of tips, this is hardly an adequate wage for an allegedly skilled worker.

In the case of the two in ten girls who go on to some sort of further education the disparities and anomalies are equally striking. Twice as many boys as girls are accepted for university places, although this is more a factor of the girls' decision than of the universities'. About half of those applying for a university place get one, whether they are boys or girls. But fewer girls than boys make the initial application. On the other hand, more girls than boys apply for places at colleges of education, where girls outnumber boys four to one. Obviously, a university degree has more market value than a qualification from a college of education, since it provides access to a wider range of professions. But even within the field of teaching, university graduates tend to be preferred to others for promotion to heads of department and to headmasterships.

The fact that women take up a third of the university places seems roughly in line with the proportion of women workers in the labour force as a whole. But the range of subjects chosen by women students often reflects a lack of interest in the realities of a marketable career. For instance, of pupils leaving school in recent years with two or more GCE 'A' level passes, only about two girls in ten specialized in science, compared with five in ten boys. Whereas on, the arts side, the percentages were practically reversed. This suggests that many girls voluntarily cut themselves off from careers in industry. It also suggests that in many cases they cut themselves off from a university training as well. In 1972 the Universities Central Council on Admissions reported that over 2000 places went unfilled, among may them in science and engineering. Thus it seems that women themselves play a part in their restriction to a small number of employments, generally at a low level of pay and of responsibility. And the fact that there are so many women competing for a limited number of jobs in a limited variety of occupations helps keep down the level of wages.

Equally significant is the choice of a job a girl makes when she leaves school. If she is to go on to further education, the subjects she studies at school will determine to a great extent the sort of employment for which she will be fitted when her student days are over. By the time a girl enters employment, the die is largely cast. Today, because of the raising of the school-leaving age to sixteen, and the earlier marriages of the majority of women, a girl has less time in which to pick up vocational skills before pregnancy compels her to give up her work. Yet, as we have seen, the fields in which most women choose to work offer far less chance of further training than do those of the men employees. How and why, then, do women acquiesce in a system in which they make up one third of the work-force, but are paid only one-fifth of the national wage bill? For acquiesce they do. It is an attitude that is proof against any law that can be devised.

In industry, women are excluded from many employments whether they want them or not. In the professions, however, women have been guaranteed access to most employments since 1919 by the Sex Disqualification (Removal) Act. And yet, over fifty years later, there was not a single woman member of the Institute of Building although, as one trade unionist said, 'we should love to have them on the scaffold'.

This situation may have developed at a time when women had little direct influence upon politics. However, since 1929 adult women have had the vote, and there are 105 women to every 100 men in this country. But it was not until 1970 that legislation, the Equal Pay Act, was secured. In the General Election of that year, twenty-six women were returned out of a total of 630 MPs. Legislation, it would seem, may have made equality a legal possibility, but it is unable to penetrate the psychological barrier of women's conditioning.

The very sad thing is that – and one tries not to admit to this, particularly if one is one of them – having taught for four years I am impressed more and more that a lot of girls are . . . 'brain-washed', but certainly by the time they are fourteen, fifteen, sixteen, they are no longer thinking beyond very narrow channels.[14]

Most of these channels lead in one direction, towards marriage. The importance of the increasingly brief period between school and marriage is often not fully grasped either by the girls themselves or by their parents. Most girls leave school to go into full-time employment. Yet many seem to regard the work that they do in that time as merely a stopgap until marriage. The big problem now is to get over the message that the work role is not an alternative to marriage: the one complements the other except for those years when, as a wife and mother, she will spend some time away from the work-place having and bringing up her children.

Another part of the problem is to decide who is best equipped to get this message across. Careers officers make the point that there are too few of them to have much effect on schoolgirls, and in any case, by the time the girls reach the careers officer, it is usually too late. The girls have already chosen to study appropriately 'feminine' arts subjects, or have been forced into doing so because many girls' schools lack science facilities. In fact, the schools themselves play a big part in the conditioning of girls to accept the role assigned to them by society. For the majority of their teachers, particularly in junior school, will be women who, as products of the process themselves, are hardly likely in large numbers to question it.

Thus we are left with the parents. But by and large society is still at a stage where we believe that education is intrinsically desirable and fail to consider in what our children are being educated. The determined parent can defy the system and get away with it, however. Mr Ted Bishop, the Labour MP, tells the story of his own daughter, who wanted to take 'A' level economics at the girls' school she was attending. She was told that economics was not on the curriculum and she had better pick another subject. Eventually, however, the school was forced to arrange for her to take classes at a boys' school. As a result, she took first-class honours in economics at university and went on to a job in accountancy, usually regarded, and for no good reason, as a men's preserve.

However, there are now some hopeful signs on the horizon for the many girls and their parents who lack such persistence, or even a thorough awareness of the problems of sex-typing. Under government pressure, inspectors of the Department of Education and Science are now studying the extent to which curricular differences contribute to unequal opportunities for boys and girls. Furthermore, girls themselves are beginning to show signs of greater competitiveness for the qualifications that intelligence alone is not enough to secure. The number of girls taking 'O' and 'A' levels in all subjects of the GCE examinations is growing faster than that of boys, especially in science, economics and English.

Hand in hand with improvements in education, however, there has to be an updating of the vocational help available to the large numbers of women returning to the labour market after their children have started school. Improvements in education will take many years to work through the system before they can bring about wiser career choices. Much of their impact will also be lost unless there is a better understanding by the girls themselves of the various stages of their lives.

At present, far too many appear unable to see beyond their wedding day or the birth of the first child. As we have seen, the period between the last child's reaching school age and the mother's official retirement age, at present sixty, is steadily increasing. For many women it is thirty years or more, when for their grandmother it might have been five. In this context, the career a woman has as a 'home-leaver' becomes almost more important than the career she had as a school-leaver. But the two are inextricably linked, for a new training is much more easily acquired if the training habit is already ingrained.

Work is compatible with marriage or motherhood. The issue is simply that these functions and the world of work have been allowed to drift apart, until they seem alternatives when they are in fact complementary. They were so once, and ought to be so again. But the big changes that are taking place in marriage patterns challenge the conventional opinion that a husband, a home, a family, and a little pin-money ought to be enough for any woman. First, the pace of modern industrial society often demands that the husband should be away from home for much of his time. Secondly, families are smaller than they used to be and consequently the children become independent earlier. On the other hand, the life expectation of the mother has considerably increased. This in turn is bringing more married women into the labour market, so the competition for the limited range of jobs available to such women can be fierce. The woman who once thought a pin-money training was all she would ever need when she left school is now facing stiffer competition than ever before.

So far, we have examined women's attitudes to work in terms of preoccupation with marriage, as a result of which the job is regarded as of secondary rather than complementary status. Alternatively, it has been agued that the lack of ambition of many women, and their apparent acceptance of low-powered jobs, may be an intelligent adjustment to the limited range of job opportunities open to them. In either case the common theme is that work is but a part of life, and possibly one of the less important.

The implications of this attitude, however, are by no means all negative. Indeed, it may be that in female attitudes to work there is a lot that could usefully be learned by many men. For just as many women resent the difficulties that are placed in their path to promotion and to responsible, interesting jobs, a similar bitterness is felt by the man who has been passed over. But he at least is spared the indignity of knowing that his sex alone was a drawback big enough to outweigh his individuality. This bears down particularly hard upon the unmarried, or childless, women. It is hard, too, on widows or deserted wives. Such women are not only deprived of the ordinary satisfactions of marriage, but also may have dependants to support.

More and more women are combining marriage and work. But many are still confined to one role or the other and we are slowly beginning to realize the cost both in terms of loss of individual potential and of the waste of skills and services to society. From the increasing numbers of women who can combine both, it may be that we are learning to put work in its proper place as an important but not necessarily paramount part of individual experience.

To give an example, certain obsolete legislation which classed women with young persons has been used to prevent women from working at night, except with special permission. Similarly, certain machinery, considered dangerous, has been regarded as unsuitable for operation by women. But these restrictions have caused people to point out that, if working at night or with certain machines is unhealthy for women it might also be unhealthy for men.

The growing importance of women in the work-force is also causing some reappraisal further up the management tree. As Professor Michael Fogarty has observed:

Restarting in middle life, flexible retirement and working at less than full pressure after age fifty-five, the shift in motivation from money and power to service and people, and the growing ten-

dency to balance work against outside interests are all current
issues for men as much as women.[15]

In discussions with managers, Professor Fogarty noted
suggestions that employers could reduce the pressure on
fathers as well as on mothers during the child-rearing period.
'But', he added, 'the managers cannot see the force which
will make it practicable in the rat-race-and-escalator pattern
of management careers as it now is.'

In this, as in so many other ways, private industry is
distinctly conservative compared with public sector employers. The Civil Service, for instance, already offers some
paternity leave to fathers. However, this is not available to
the Civil Service's industrial employees. These, unlike the
non-industrial service, belong to unions other than Civil
Service associations and are therefore subject to collective
agreements under which women have an inferior position
to men. The recently retired Head of the Home Civil Service,
Sir William Armstrong, has already noted a shift in attitudes
among young men entering service. 'The young men now
coming into the service have a totally different attitude . . .
towards their wife and towards their home as well as a
totally different attitude towards women generally.'[16] Sir
William gave an example of a young couple in which the
man was employed in the Diplomatic Service and the woman
in the Home Office. Rather than take up an overseas post,
the husband transferred to the Home Service, because the
move would have deprived his wife of the years that she
would lose if he went abroad. Until the war, this would have
been 'very extraordinary', Sir William added. Today, it was
'widely approved of as the sensible way for a man to behave'.

Professor Fogarty sees a range of options with the balance
of work and non-work interests varying even more strongly
than now from family to family. This in turn will make for
more complex problems both for mother, father and personnel manager in terms of recruitment, transfers and promo-

tions. But if the growing involvement of women, particularly mothers, in the work-place is accompanied by a growing involvement of fathers in the home, then there are many who would say that this would be no bad thing.

8. Work's attitudes to women

Insofar as differences [of ability] between men and women are real, they are a matter of statistical probability, not of a difference between all women and all men. Differences between individuals of either sex far outweigh them in importance.

Michael Fogarty

In January 1972 Mr Isaac Donner, the managing director of a shirtmakers' company was reported as saying that he wanted to replace with men the 1400 women in his company's factories in Yorkshire and in Wales.[1] The company employed about 100 men at this time. Mr Donner's reasons for this decision throw an interesting light on the attitudes of employers to women workers.

Basically, they amounted to this: in four years' time the Equal Pay Act of 1970 would come into force, obliging him to pay his women workers the same as the men where engaged upon 'the same or broadly similar work'. In other words, the women's work would become dearer. Secondly, he was reported to have said, 'Having trained them, we are just not getting our money's worth.' Girls, he said, had at one time joined the firm on leaving school at the age of fourteen and stayed at work until they got married at about twenty. Now the school-leaving age was sixteen, and the girls were marrying at eighteen or nineteen, thus halving their period of usefulness to the company. Thirdly, new machines were being brought into the garment trade. These were very expensive but allowed the work to be done as well by men as by women, who formerly had an edge because of their greater manual dexterity.

But in order to earn their keep, the machines had to be worked over two or three shifts, and legislation prevented women from working at night. 'With equal pay coming soon I will be employing all the men I can get,' Mr Donner said.

There, neatly encapsulated, we have three recurring strands in employers' attitudes to women as workers. They are, first, that women are of limited value as employees because of their protected status under the law; secondly, that their usefulness and their eligibility for training are further lessened by the short, and diminishing, period between leaving school for work and leaving work for children; thirdly, that the combination of the first and second reasons makes men more valuable as employees, except where women are cheaper.

The knot that gathers these strands together is the associated assumption that women, unlike men, are to be classed as members of a sex rather than as individuals. In other words, when a man applies for a job he will by and large be judged according to his qualities of intelligence or aptitude. A woman, on the other hand, must first and foremost be considered as belonging to a sex whose members habitually leave employment for maternal duties. If the woman is already a wife and mother, her position will be even less favourable, for it will be assumed that these functions will automatically take precedence over her role as a worker.

She is sure to quit her job altogether if her husband moves out of the district, and take time off during school holidays or a domestic crisis. To make matters worse, in the present scheme of things employers tend to be men, and so exhibit current prejudices as to what jobs are either seemly for a woman or fitted to contemporary estimates of female capacities. Typical of such attitudes is the comment of an employer in insurance, an occupation where women out-number men but are mostly employed at the lower levels. Asked about higher-level opportunities for women, he said, 'Well, we have solicitors, but of course this is very difficult work and women would not want to do it.'[2]

Then there is the attitude which designates certain jobs as unsuitable for women, rather than as unsuitable for all, most, or some women, 'Even if a woman wants to do the job you would still say "I don't think you want to do that." We know that some women do very heavy work – in Russia you see them on the roads. I would not like to employ women on the roads.'[3] Setting aside for the moment the possibility that women are by their nature inherently less valuable employees than men, one question must be asked right away: what about the women who do not conform to the pattern that society has mapped out for them? What of the women who do not marry, do not leave the labour force, do not have the protection of a man's wages packet?

This habit of thinking of women as members of a sex rather than as individuals penalizes the unmarried, the divorced, the widowed, and the deserted. According to Mr Donner's rule, such women, on leaving school, are denied training, promotion and even employment, in precisely the same way as the girl who leaves work permanently upon marriage. And for 150 years they have been denied equal pay but not equal responsibilities, as well as the support of children and possibly of parents. Such women have another burden, which most men are spared, of responsibility for the housekeeping.

This attitude is one that has grown up among employers only in proportion as it has permeated society at large. It is to be found, as we shall see, in the law, in the attitude of male workmates, and not least among women themselves. It is in fact present in all the elements that go to make up working life. Thus society's failure to respect the individuality of women is not only wrong. It is also harmful in its effect upon a large and increasingly important section of the work-force.

Why has this habit grown up, and how does it contrast with the present situation, in which women, and particularly married women, are the faster growing component of the employed population? The essence of habit is absence of thought, and it is only in the last few years that we as an industrial nation have really got down to thinking out the issues involved in the employment outside the home of large and growing numbers of women. Many people would argue that the trouble with industrial society is that it treats nobody as individuals, be they men or women. Such a view begins to appear credible when, for instance, one considers the position of car-workers, who work in totally automated, compartmentalized and mass-production conditions, and whose fortunes, were it not for crippling strikes, are largely governed from Detroit, a city they have never seen. They work in large buildings and against a din that drains individuality from any human being.

This is true enough, but the effects of industrial society on women have been far deeper. First, such attitudes act to prevent full use being made of women's abilities, to the benefit of themselves as individuals and of the economy. Secondly, they actually discourage women from entering employment, for two-thirds of married women still do not return to work. The large numbers of women affected make this an important consideration, for almost all girls in the United Kingdom take paid work on leaving full-time education, unlike their counterparts in the Netherlands and, to a lesser extent in France, where more unmarried girls stay at home or work in the family farm or business. Lastly, there is the wide range of jobs over which such attitudes hold sway. Baroness Seear, for example, reports[4] that when senior managers in eight companies were asked what jobs were unsuitable for a woman, they produced a 'fairly lengthy list'. On closer scrutiny it was found that 'in nearly every case a job mentioned as unsuitable for a woman in one company was in fact being done elsewhere by a woman'.

In 1965 a government social survey reported that of twenty types of work undertaken by women only one involved training lasting more than six months. Probably three-quarters of employed women are in jobs that take less than six months to learn. Conversely, most employers' experience of women employees has been at the lower levels of responsibility. Yet the Confederation of British Industry, the employers' pressure group, concedes that 'levels of responsibility appear to have at least as great an effect on turnover and absenteeism as sex'.[5]

How far, then, is the behaviour of working women representative of feminine nature, and, how far of low-paid, unskilled, poorly motivated workers of either sex? This is the question that is now increasingly being asked, both by employers and by women themselves. Common sense would seem to dictate that the answer is: not as much to do with feminine nature as male employers think, and not as little as the more enthusiastic say. However, nobody knows, for nobody has yet made it their business to sort out the matter in a way that would convince both sides. There just is not the evidence. But the absence of proof has not served to deter employers from sometimes making the most sweeping of assumptions.

Mr Donner gave as one of his reasons for preferring men to women as workers the legislation which restricted women's working at night. Indeed, no study of work's attitudes to women can be made without reference to the impact of legislation. It is the law, after all, that regulates the conditions under which employers may offer work to men or women. To the extent that the law hedges the employment of women around with special provisions, it will load the scales one way or the other in an employer's decision to hire, fire or promote a woman rather than a man.

There are, however, other aspects of legislation that have served to put women workers at a disadvantage. A law which grants women a special status will handicap some women though it may be intended to protect them from strains likely to affect their functions as wives and mothers. But there is also the sort of law which, in adopting a neutral line towards the special problems of women, in fact serves only to perpetuate existing injustice and inefficient use of women's labour. As an example of the latter, there is the Industrial Training Act of 1964, which created a network of industrial training boards with responsibility for about 15 million workers, over half the employed population. At the time that the Act was passed it, was a new and exciting initiative, for the new law signified 'the general acceptance of the relatively new concept that training is for the benefit of the industry rather than for the benefit of the employer who provides it'.

Or to put it another way, the Act signified government impatience with industry's preference for poaching trained personnel from other firms rather than for investing in the training of its own employees. But if the Act was for the benefit of industry, there was remarkably little evidence that it was for the benefit of women. It may be that in 1964 there was even less appreciation than today of the developing problem in women's employment, namely that more and more women were coming into the labour market, particularly married women, at a time when the opportunities open to them were not expanding on the same scale. In fact it was not until a year later, with the publication of the National Plan, that there was an attempt to isolate the female labour force as the last available reserve of labour.

Be that as it may, the industrial training boards were not out to challenge any employer's assumptions. First, two training boards for office work and hairdressing were quickly killed. These were meant to cover industries in which women outnumbered men. As we have seen, in office work most girls are expected to train themselves out of office hours. And in hairdressing, the 'training' given by many employers is merely a euphemism for the cheap labour of giving shampoos and sweeping out the shop.

Secondly, the remaining boards catered by and large for industries, such as distributive trades and engineering, where women were not doing skilled work and therefore were denied opportunities for further training. Thirdly, the boards were not required to provide separate statistics for the numbers of men and women under training, with the result that they did not even offer any useful information in lieu of increased training for women. The Act, like the society that produced it, and like much of the legislation that had gone before, embodied the general assumption that paid employment was of peripheral importance to the main business of a woman's life, her home and family.

So far as women were concerned, therefore, the Act merely served to bolster the existing inequality in training opportunities between men and women. Under the Act, money was collected from a levy on payroll and repaid in grants for training undertaken. But the aim was only to make it easier for employers to train those they wanted to train, which in most cases did not include women. The levy was collected on the male as well as the female payroll. Since there was little evidence of any increase in the training given women, it seems probable that the money thus generated was used not only without any intention of helping women, but actually to subsidize the training of men at the expense of women.

Training was also made available through Government Training Centres. In January 1973 4000 women were undergoing training compared with 29 000 men. However, most of the women's places were not in the GTCs as such, but in commercial colleges offering approved courses. Most of the courses offered at the GTCs were in construction and engineering, industries which have a poor record for either attracting women or permitting them to train. Little was done to encourage women to look beyond the customary clerical work. There was an effort neither to persuade women to sign up for courses which otherwise they would not have considered, nor to help those women who independently had arrived at such a decision.

Nowhere was official blindness to the situation of women more manifest than in the financial help available under the GTC scheme. Men and women at nineteen could both qualify for an allowance of £9·50 a week, but at twenty or over the man got £11·75 and the woman £10·75. When allowances were increased, the men got another 50p a week and the women 30p. This discrimination was manifestly absurd, for in the first place women's need for training was at least as great as, if not greater than, that of men's.

Secondly, although the travelling expenses of both sexes from home to the centre would be identical, the woman was far more likely to need hired help for her children while she was taking her course. Both examples of 'negative' legislation chosen have been to do with training, for it is here that the magnitude of the problem posed by employers' attitudes and the inadequacy of the legislative response are seen most clearly.

Let us now consider the training offered through day-release and apprenticeships. Although there has recently been pressure for change, day-release training which is not usually entirely vocational, has not been mandatory. In 1973, only 10·4 per cent of young women in employment were receiving day-release, compared with 39·7 per cent of young men. Furthermore, the industries in which women got the least day-release were those in which the highest proportion were employed, the amount ranging from 2·1 per cent in clothing and footwear to 3·7 per cent in paper, publishing and printing. The case of day-release is particularly serious, for the non-vocational element in the training is designed to help those young people who have left school at the minimum leaving age to overcome some of the ensuing educational handicaps.

If we turn to apprenticeships, the position is even worse. In May 1970 there were 110 women apprentices to skilled craft occupations, compared to 112 000 men. Of the girls who take up apprenticeships, three-quarters are in hairdressing. Over a third of girl school-leavers go into clerical work, and two-thirds of clerical workers are women. However, the Commercial and Clerical Training Committee of the Central Training Council was allowed to lapse in 1969, and in its absence no appropriate industrial training board was set up. 'It is a continuing source of amazement', noted a TUC study, 'that an occupation undertaken by so many women – and which makes an essential contribution to the efficiency of every undertaking – is still not generally recognized as requiring an industrial apprenticeship.'[6]

If we move on from negative to what might be called 'positive' legislation, or laws that actively seek to confer upon women a special status and to protect that status from harm caused by 'unsuitable' forms of paid employment, then we are again faced with ineffectiveness in improving women's lot, albeit a well-intentioned ineffectiveness. The principal activity of such legislation consists of prescribing the hours during which women may work, and placing restrictions on the length of a woman's working life.

Under the National Insurance Act, the retirement age for women has been put at sixty as opposed to sixty-five for men, and this is also reflected in many private pension schemes. The reason for this difference is obscure, especially since women now live longer than men, but its effect is to encourage women to retire earlier than men. In the case of a married woman returning to work after bringing up her children her period of usefulness to the firm is thus shorter than a man's. There are also other, possibly more unfortunate, effects. One is that a woman's pension entitlements are often lower than a man's because she is likely to live longer.

Fewer women than men belong to pension schemes, usually because of the break in working life after marriage. The result is that a woman can look forward to a much longer existence upon the scant comforts of an old age pension than a man.

For many years employers have been required to pay full social security contributions whenever an employee had worked more than eight hours in any one week. Although this legislation was not specifically brought in to discriminate against women, it has the effect of doing so. The reason is that women, more than men, seek part-time work. About half the married women in the work-force work part-time, for example, since they find this fits in best with their domestic responsibilities. In some employments, this makes it more economic to employ one worker full-time rather than two part-time. Thus, where two married women might have found employment, the job is more likely to go to neither of them.

However, the largest single source of complaint from employers springs from restrictions upon the hours in which women may work. In 1844 the legal restrictions on the hours of young children in textile mills, introduced eleven years earlier, were extended to include women. There are at the moment general restrictions on the hours of employment of women manual workers in premises covered by Part IV of the Factories Act 1961. These limit the maximum number of hours a woman may work to forty-eight (although this is in fact more than the average number now worked by men). The main bone of contention with the employers is the Act's insistence that these hours must not start before 7 a.m. nor finish after 8 p.m. Mr Donner's grievance then becomes clear, for to make his machinery pay it would be necessary to work shifts that might cut across these limits. In practice, emergency legislation left over from the last war allows for exemption to be obtained for individual firms for the purpose of maintaining or increasing efficiency which, of course, allows a wide latitude. Once granted, the exemptions are 'almost invariably renewed'.

Legislation restricting hours of work, though to some extent reflecting the antagonism between the landed aristocracy and the newly rich manufacturers, was based upon the assumption that such long hours were a danger to the main business of a woman's life, running a home and bearing children. It was in these mills and factories that we first saw the emergence of large numbers of women as workers in paid employment outside the home. But it was many years before legislative attention was paid to women in more ladylike trades. The situation of women working in the garment trades, at home, in the warrens of the cities, or living-in in the fashionable London shops, was not satisfactorily regulated until the turn of this century.

Even at the time when protection was being extended to factory women, the women themselves feared it would have the effect of making tnem less acceptable as employees. They were conscious that some reformers would like to exclude them from the new industrial employment altogether, arguing that with the departure of cheap labour, a man would have to be paid enough to support a whole family.

It is a lamentable fact [noted the Female Operatives of Todmorden during this debate] that, in these parts of the country, there is scarcely any other mode of employment for female industry, if we except servitude [domestic service] and dressmaking. Of the former of these, there is no chance of employment for one twentieth of the candidates that would rush into the field, to say nothing of lowering the wages of our sisters in the same craft: and of the latter, galling as some of the hardships are (of which the indelicacy of mixing with the men is not the least) yet there are few women who have been so employed that would change conditions with the ill-used genteel little slaves who have to lose sleep and health in catering to the whims and frivolities of the butterflies of fashion.[7]

In the 1850s William Acton, a doctor, wrote:

If we compare the prostitute at thirty-five with her sister, who perhaps is the married mother of a family, or has been the toiling slave for years in the over-heated laboratories of fashion, we shall seldom find that the constitutional ravages often thought to be the necessary consequence of prostitution exceed those attributable to the cares of a family and the heart-wearing struggles of virtuous labour.[8]

Today it is probable that the Factories Acts affect only about a quarter of the female work-force, and even here the average number of hours worked by women in industry is about forty, eight less than the law allows. In late 1973 the government announced proposals to repeal this legislation. A review, published four years earlier, had shown that, outside factories, the only places where women's hours were statutorily regulated were in shops, mines and quarries. 'Thus,' the report continued, 'while a woman cannot normally be employed after 8 p.m. in a factory, if she becomes a nurse, a bus conductress or a waitress she can be employed until any hour of the night or, indeed all night.'[9]

The proposal to repeal this legislation was part of a package aimed at making unlawful the discrimination between men and women in employment and education on grounds of sex.

Legislation was felt to be necessary to increase the range of job opportunities open to women. The task was then especially urgent, for, as we have seen with Mr Donner, the enforcement in 1976 of the Equal Pay Act of 1970 would make some employers reluctant to keep on women in some traditional female occupations. It was all the more necessary, therefore, to make sure that alternative opportunities were at hand. An added value of such legislation, it was argued, was that it would help employers who were unwilling to discriminate but felt bound by social pressures.

In the 1970s, for example, London Transport found itself short of several train and bus drivers, with the result that services had to be cut. The authority was willing to offer driving jobs to women, and there were women able and willing to do the work. Indeed women had been driving London suburban buses for years, and had handled everything from ambulances to Liberator bombers in the war. The union, the Transport and General, was also willing to admit women as drivers, but the proposal had to be put to members at branch level, who for a long time promptly and repeatedly refused.

Such attitudes, rather than the differences of aptitude between men and women, often prove decisive. In 1972, for example, the case of Cable and Wireless Limited, a nationalized company, was brought to the attention of the House of Lords Select Committee on the second Anti-Discrimination Bill. This company advertised for recruits in telecommunications engineering, the necessary qualifications being five GCE 'O' levels, with preference being given to holders of two 'A' level subjects. A girl wrote in, who not only had twelve 'O' levels, including the required subjects, but also was about to take three 'A' levels. One of the reasons she was turned down was that there were no separate lavatories at the residential training centre. The cleaners, presumably women, no doubt waited until they got home. The fact that the girl was obviously far brighter than the average recruit was in no way allowed to offset the central objection that she was a woman.

Another example of this attitude was provided by Mr E. C. Jones, director of personnel at Smiths Industries, a firm employing 11 000 women. Mr Jones's evidence to the Select Committee was a fine example of this automatic readiness to generalize about women while particularizing about men.

We have a ceramics division where there are ovens which operate at a very high temperature. There may be the exception, but generally speaking experience has persuaded us not to attempt to employ women within the area of these ovens, because they are unable physically to sustain an effort over the period of the given shift. The rest periods they require become more frequent and so there is discrimination in favour of the females, if you like. We tend to prevent them from working in this excessive heat.[1]

Now, while this observation may be taken as evidence that men are better able than women to stand the heat in Smiths oven room, Mr Jones had apparently moved on to conclude that the job should be closed to all women, even though 'there may be the exception' who could stand the heat, and might want the job. While men might, on balance, be better suited to this admittedly unpleasant job than women, it does not follow either that all men could stand the heat or that some, admittedly fewer, women were not better able to stand it than some men. Furthermore, if a job has ill effects on some, but not all, women, and on some, but fewer, men, why should this be grounds for closing the job to all women? If the same reasoning were applied to men, the fact that some individuals were unable to complete a shift comfortably would be grounds for closing the job to all men. As it is, presumably any man who can show that he can go the distance can have the job, although any woman is automatically barred, whether or not she has the capacity for the work.

9. Women and the professions today: too little, too late

In selecting for a professional or managerial job it is very nearly true to say that one knows nothing worth knowing if one knows only that one candidate is a woman and another is a man. There is no ability or set of attitudes characteristic of many women which is not also characteristic of many men, and vice versa.

Michael Fogarty

Women outnumber men in two professions: medicine and education. In these, they have achieved equal pay, but not equal access to training and therefore to promotion. In medicine, nine out of ten nurses are women, but only one qualified doctor in four is a woman. Many women doctors do not practise medicine, for even though the National Health Service is short of doctors, the profession is unwilling to provide the opportunities of part-time work that would enable women to combine family commitments with a return to work. Thus, despite the fact that a quarter of qualified doctors are women, the number actually practising is much lower. In 1970, 14 per cent of hospital staff doctors were women, and only 12·2 per cent of general practitioners. There are also complaints that fewer women than before are being appointed to senior medical posts.

If we turn to dentistry, the proportions are lower still,

E

being respectively 8·5 and 7·3 per cent. In teaching, only 15 per cent of the staff in higher education are women, although women outnumber men in the schools. Again, there are complaints that fewer and fewer women are being appointed to headships and to run departments in schools.

Women do seem to be losing ground in 'their' professions even where in the recent past they may even have enjoyed slightly more favourable treatment than men. In nursing, for example, men have been prevented by law from being midwives, which in practice also prevents men from gaining a health visitor's certificate, since a prerequisite for this qualification is training in midwifery and obstetric nursing. By custom, rather than by law, women have been preferred to men in the staffing and direction of primary and girls' schools. The lower status and pay in primary education made this area less attractive to men, and in the case of girls' schools many parents prefer female staff. Until long after the last war women teachers were paid less than men, so local authorities were only too happy to indulge this parental whim. In 1971, although more women than men were in teaching, only one in five head teachers in primary and secondary schools was a woman. In 1973, the general secretary of the National Union of Teachers said that since equal pay for teachers had been introduced eight years earlier, the number of women headmistresses had fallen by 2000.

In teaching as in medicine, two factors are helping to erode the advances made by women over the past century. One is the balancing out of the sexes in the population, which has increased young women's chances of marriage, and therefore decreased the number of single women able to pursue an unbroken career. Secondly, the changes in organization that are taking place, particularly in the schools, are tending to merge girls' and boys' schools into single, large units, headed by a man. Even Roedean now has a male head.

Professional women are now more likely than ever before

to get married, and leave either to have their children or when their husbands are offered promotion in another district. The situation is worsened by the local authorities' habit of generalizing from the particular. Since the last war, they have been advertising some posts as for men only, as though all men were inherently more suitable than any woman for the post in question, an obvious nonsense. In medicine, according to careers officers, more talented girls would like to become doctors and veterinarians than have courage to apply to the university medical schools because of 'this tradition that there is professional rejection of all but the ablest girls'.[1]

This pre-selection by the girls themselves appears to be as important a factor in limiting their access to jobs in medicine as the attitudes of the medical schools themselves. 'In 1966', said the dean of a London hospital, 'we studied all of the incoming medical students in the country, and all of the [medical] schools showed that their girl entrants had been faced with much more opposition, particularly at school but to some extent at home', before they could get into medicine.[2]

Others would argue that this discouragement was no more than the justifiable reaction to the discriminatory policies of medical schools. There were, for example, no women at all in the London medical schools until 1948, when their paymasters, the University Grants Committee, insisted upon a quota of 15 per cent of total admissions. By 1972 a third of the students in medical schools were girls, about the same proportion as the number of women to men applicants. At four hospitals, however, a self-imposed quota remained. This varied from 25 per cent of intake at the Charing Cross Hospital, London, to about a third at Dundee University. On the basis of these quotas, it was common practice for men to be admitted in preference to women with better results at GCE 'A' level.

Yet in medicine marriage is still allowed to stifle as many

women's careers as the discrimination of the deans of medical schools. Less than a third of the country's women doctors work full-time, half work part-time, and a fifth not at all. The medical profession, like many others, tends to view marriage on the part of its women members as evidence of a faulty sense of vocation. But in fact there is not enough part-time work available in the right places to enable many women doctors with young children to resume practice. Where there are vacancies, the pay is often too low to make working worthwhile. It may hardly cover the cost of home help, where this is available. An attempt to circularize over 100 Birmingham women doctors once found less than ten able or willing to go back to work.

The last war looms large in any discussion of the problems of women doctors. On the one hand, that war proved beyond a doubt the folly of regarding women as merely supportive workers. On the other hand, as the idea of following a profession became more commonplace, so it became harder to achieve. Home help became scarce, as the pre-war legions of domestic servants left for the factories, never to return. And their memories of the service were such as to persuade their daughters and grand-daughters to stay clear of another woman's parlour.

After the war, also, the number of medical school places that the country would need was underestimated and the resultant pressure on these places from applicants, and shortage of doctors in the NHS have bolstered male privileges. Doctors, surprisingly considering their professional interest in the reproductive function, find its operation among women to be sufficient reason for exclusion from medical schools. 'If we train 100 men,' said one medical administrator, 'then in five or ten years' time we shall have 100 doctors in full-time practice; if we train 100 women, then we shall have only 30 per cent working in five or ten years, and then most probably in part-time work.'[3]

Why this should be so, how far it is a fact of nature and

how far a product of the profession's insensitivity, or even whether some of the women lost are better doctors than the men who remain, are questions which still await satisfactory diagnosis.

In teaching, the decreasing competitiveness of women with men is to a greater degree due to over-production of graduates since the last war. John Holloway, of the University of Manchester's Careers and Appointments Service, has pointed out that as high a proportion of the population is now taking degrees as twenty-five years ago was taking school certificates.

As we have seen, over twice as many girls as boys go to colleges of education rather than to universities, even though girls' 'A' level results are at least as good as boys'. This leaves girls at an initial disadvantage for their reliance upon teaching is increased by industry's reluctance to regard qualifications from the colleges of education as evidence of anything other than a preparation for teaching. Boys, however, have been increasingly driven to consider teaching as a career by fluctuations in other careers opportunities for graduates. In teaching as in industry, however, a degree is a bigger door-opener than a teaching certificate. The prejudices of local education authorities in making appointments and promotions see to the rest. Therefore the proportion of men to women in school-teaching is 42:58, but in the lowest grade posts it is 24:76, and in the highest 60:40. In 1972 there were only forty-four women professors out of a national total of 3200, half of which were in one university, London.

In the schools, teachers are beginning to talk of the necessity of drawing distinctions between 'career' teachers and the rest, meaning, in practice, between men and women. The concept is dangerously close to the prejudice, already discussed, that women have one set of attitudes and men another, as a result of which women need not be regarded as individuals. In part, the frustration of many men teachers is understandable, for the preponderance of women in the profession for many years held back brisk union activity and therefore advances in salary and status. However, a consciousness of inferior treatment among women eventually becomes self-fulfilling, as we have seen in medicine. Women begin not to apply for promotion, or worse still, drift into other work or no work at all after their children have grown up. It is a rich irony, indeed, that this sex-typing should happen in a profession whose basis is respect for the individual. It is another that the women in this profession who have for so long acquiesced in the conditioning of their girl pupils against challenging bastions of male privilege, should now find their own about to fall. 'If it is becoming difficult or atypical for women to become leaders of traditionally female professions,' says the Institute of Careers Officers, 'then the likelihood is that there will be a mood of less acceptability in traditionally male professions.'[4]

In 1972 the Royal Institute of British Architects published a survey which showed the proportion of women members of professional institutes. If we look at twenty of these associations, we find that women's membership ranges from nil in the Institute of Building (20 964 men) to 17·8 per cent, or 8863 women in the British Medical Association (49 714 men). In only one other body, the British Dental Association, did their membership exceed 10 per cent. The architects themselves, for instance, could muster only 4·2 per cent, and the Institute of Bankers, where the female labour force outnumbers the male, produced a total of 1·2 per cent. The figure was less than 2 per cent for the chartered accountants, for solicitors, chartered surveyors, town planners and even the chartered secretaries and administrators. Yet the legal right to enter most professions was granted women over half a century before, by the Sex Disqualification (Removal) Act of 1919, which laid down that neither sex nor marriage should disqualify a woman from carrying on any civil profession. The Act, in theory, at least ended an exclusion that had lasted ever since the professions began to organize themselves during the last century, and was based upon long terms of professional education, to university standard.

Since secondary education became compulsory for both sexes, girls have learned more than the governess's 'accomplishments' already mentioned, but still not enough to make the fullest use of their new opportunities. For from the beginning the aim has been to prepare girls only for 'such professions as women might be fitted to fill'. In practice, this means teaching, social work or, to stretch a point, medicine. Before 1919 and the Sex Discrimination (Removal) Act, women were excluded from a wide range of professions by the whim of male practitioners and by the widespread denial of effective secondary education. Today, boys' and girls' career possibilities diverge almost as widely thanks to the timidity and the compliant outlook of the new girls' schools. Although for some years the trend has been towards co-education, it will be much longer before our society overcomes the effects of fifty years of separate schools, cheerfully and unthinkingly instilling a narrow range of characteristics and of aspirations.

Thus, in 1970, half a century after the law had given women access to professions, prejudice ensured that many, such as accountancy, remained virtually closed to women. The situation in that profession has been ably analysed by Sheila Masters, who signed her articles in 1970 and subsequently won an examination prize of the Institute of Taxation. 'The accountant,' she wrote, 'naturally a cautious person, argues that he cannot be certain of recouping the cost of training women since they leave in order to get married.'

Even those who returned were regarded by the men as having shown a lack of dedication to the career.

There is, I think, a confusion between career and profession. A woman's basic drives may not be as strongly devoted to pursuing a scintillating career, but this does not negate the possibility of her playing an important, though less spectacular, part in her profession. The accountancy profession is large enough to accommodate all kinds of accountants, not the least of which should be the woman accountant, whether or not she has a strong career instinct.[5]

Such, however is the temper not only of accountancy but of company secretaryship, personnel management, banking, insurance, office management and all the new disciplines that owe their recent accretion of influence to the development of the company system.

An insidious chain reaction now operates, set off by the professions' discouragement of potential female entrants. The theme is then taken up by kindly teachers, more often than not women, who, wanting to spare their charges disappointment, prepare them for nice, ladylike employments – like teaching. The professions are unlikely to advertise in girls' schools. Or if they do, the literature will usually contain reference to and pictures of men. Because few women have in the past made it into the professional ranks outside teaching, there will be little in the way of refresher courses and part-time work for women returning after having or rearing children. This in turn discourages yet more girls from taking up a profession outside the 'ghetto' jobs, and by ensuring a high fall-out rate among those women who try to combine a career with marriage, provides the professions with further pretexts for postponing the day when sensible arrangements shall be made. In the meantime, the learned institutes may piously and rightly contend that they operate no formal bar to women: not enough girls leave school with the right sort of qualifications.

10. Married women: burying the talents

Man's love is of man's life a thing apart,
'Tis woman's whole existence.

Byron, Don Juan

A woman can be the most perfect wife, but her chances of being divorced in the future are greatly increased. Therefore we must change our attitudes towards girls. We must ensure that they are trained to do some job other than that of marriage.

Baroness Summerskill

Few women fare worse in the present employment situation than working mothers. In no area of the labour market is there a greater waste of potential both in the numbers of workers available and in the range of their talents. Increasingly, the story of women's employment in our time is going to be that of the employment of married women. The response of employers, of government, and not least of the wives themselves to the problems faced by married women in paid employment will largely determine the course of events in women's employment as a whole.

In recent times, the idea of married women working outside the home has been seen as a novelty, desirable or otherwise, but scarcely as part of normal working experience. Primarily, this novelty has been associated with misfortune, personal or national. In the Second World War, the UK drafted married women into the war effort both to increase the production of munitions and to fill jobs in the transport system vacated by men who had gone to fight. In peacetime,

women have always worked, although never in such numbers
as now.

Before the last war, women went out to work because their
husbands were unemployed, ill or improvident. As late as
1931, only one woman worker in ten was married. Except
in wartime, therefore, the married woman worker has been
an object of pity or of curiosity, but not of serious attention.
Today, although fewer than 50 per cent of women return to
work after having children, over six women workers in ten
are married and the proportion is still rising. A big change
is taking place, the nature and extent of which has yet to be
firmly grasped in this country.

Today's married women return to work not only for the
money but for companionship and for an escape from labour-
saving homes. They represent the only remaining sizeable
reservoir of labour available to the British economy, yet
Britain has slipped far behind other industrialized countries
in making it easier for women to leave work to have children,
and to return later to jobs reflecting their individual skills.
In 1968 the National Plan predicted a slowing down in the
annual rate of increase in the employed population from
about 0·6 per cent to about 0·25 per cent. Among the reasons
were the tapering-off of the postwar bulge of young people
entering the labour force, increases in the numbers of full-
time education, and earlier retirements. With nearly all
school-leavers, male or female, going straight into full-time
employment after finishing their education, the only substantial reserve of labour was married women. Between
1951 and 1971, the labour force increased by about 1½
million to about 25 million, an increase attributable in all
but 69 000 to the increased numbers of married women
re-entering employment. But Britain, alone among the
principal combatants of the Second World War in con-
scripting single and married women into the labour force,
is failing to adjust to this change in the composition of the
working population.

A working mother's problems begin long before she is either a mother or a worker. At school and at home she will be dissuaded from seeking work that involves much training, lest this ends at the time she wishes to marry or to have her first child. We have seen how, as a single girl, she is more likely than the single boy to be denied the opportunity of an apprenticeship, day-release or any other form of training or further education. Where the teacher is likely to argue that the training will go to waste so far as the girl herself is concerned, the employer will say that in the diminishing time between school-leaving age and that of marriage he is unlikely to recoup his investment in the training. And it must be admitted that many girls happily accept these propositions, unaware that they are likely to be back at work within ten years of marriage, but competing in a diminishing market for unskilled labour with an increasing number of their own kind as well as with school-leavers who are both younger and free of home and family commitments. On attempting to return to work, the married women also find a shortage of part-time work, except in areas of high employment, and a lack of specialized vocational guidance.

Another, perhaps more important obstacle to the married woman is the traditional British attitude to maternity leave. Alone of the developed industrial economies of Western Europe, the United Kingdom (and the Republic of Ireland), lacks any legislation to protect a woman's employment in any way during pregnancy, nor is the employer under any obligation to keep her job open after the child is born.[1] At best there are written agreements in government and local authority employments, and many private employers have reasonably generous informal policies for women non-manual workers.

But the fact remains that a woman who leaves work to have a baby is required as often as not to re-apply for her job, even if she returns to her former employer. If he takes her, it need not be in the job she left. She may lose her previous seniority, and with it pay level, holiday entitlement, sickness benefit and place in the penson scheme. She may also lose her previous period of continuous service for redundancy purposes and may have to work another 104 weeks before she regains her previous redundancy entitlement. Incomes Data found in a 1973 survey of seventy-four private companies that only eighteen had written policies on maternity leave and only six provided maternity pay.

The effect of this deficiency in the law and in employers attitudes, therefore has been to discourage women from returning to work after childbearing, or to exclude them from jobs fitted to individual abilities. Part of the problem is due to the peculiar attitude of the British toward childbearing. In some countries childbearing is seen as the means by which mother and father achieve an individual fulfilment, while discharging a responsibility to the state in keeping it peopled with a new generation of potential workers and taxpayers. The British, in contrast, seem to regard childbearing as either an illness or as evidence of lack of loyalty to the employer's cause on the part of a working woman. Most company schemes in Britain count pregnancy against sick pay entitlement.

As with so many things British, caste attitudes are also involved, since, according to British company practice in relation to pregnancy, the system favours white-collar as opposed to manual workers. The latter often have less than thirteen weeks' entitlement to sick leave at full pay, while the former may have several months' full entitlement soon after joining the firm. This is all the more ridiculous when it considered that, after West Germany, Britain has the higher proportion of economically active women in Western Europe the United States or Canada.

In the UK, however, a woman's reproductive function not seen as totally mischievous. A lump sum of £25 (1973 is payable to a woman, provided she or the father has paid twenty-six National Insurance Stamps in the appropriate

ear. A working woman may, if she is in benefit, receive an
llowance of up to £6·75 a week for eighteen weeks, starting
n the eleventh week before the expected birth. Thereafter
is a straight fight between her and her previous or prospec-
ve employer, for here, unlike in other countries, the state
trows upon the employer the onus and therefore the cost
f making up the difference between her earnings before and
ter leaving work.

Elsewhere, the pattern is for the level of earnings to be
aintained through the state insurance system, the state
iving specified the minimum benefits obtainable. In France,
a employer is not allowed to dismiss a woman during
egnancy and maternity, and she has the right to be rein-
ated for up to a year. In Italy, there is a statutory twenty
eeks' paid maternity leave, plus six months' optional leave,
d entitlement to paid leave for a child's sickness. In the
K, however, the expense of child rearing is more the
ployer's responsibility than the state's, with the result
at women become less attractive as employees.

Another discouragement to an early return to work for
any women is the shortage of nursery accommodation.
effect, this means that many mothers must wait until their
st or youngest child is five, old enough to go to primary
ool, before being able to work outside the home. Of the
v nurseries available, most are provided by firms operating
areas of full employment and therefore forced to tap
reservoir of unused labour constituted by mothers of
ung children. Many nurseries set up during the last war
ve been allowed to close. The number of day nurseries did
t rise between 1947 and 1969. Over a third of the country's
rseries are in London and the Home Counties. With such
ssure on the number of places, many day nurseries have
give preference to the children of one-parent families or of
thers in full-time work. In any event, nursery schools do not
er the school holidays and, unlike in France or the United
tes, there are few residential summer camps to reduce

the pressure on working mothers during the long summer
vacation.

The reasons underlying these changes are partly social
and partly demographic. One is the surplus of men over
women in the age group between twenty and thirty, which
makes it more likely that a girl will marry. Another is the
earlier onset of puberty, which now occurs at about fourteen
for girls and fifteen for boys, in each case a year sooner than
at the turn of the century.

It was about the time of the Boer War that the British
began to consider health as a national rather than a local
concern. The Crimean War had demonstrated that the British
soldier had less to fear from the enemy than from the inability
of the Army to heal, shelter or feed him. The Boer War
perhaps did an even greater service: it showed how puny were
the lower orders of the British towns after an Industrial
Revolution which had turned their country into the richest
in the history of the world. By 1899 the standard of physique
asked of recruits by the Army was at its lowest since Water-
loo. Yet of 12 000 men who presented themselves at Manchester 8 000 were rejected out of hand and a mere 1 200 were
fit enough to serve. Politicians were mindful that another
war, this time with France or Germany, was brewing. Such
a war would involve millions of troops and millions more in
the factories. Yet about a third of the population, it was
discovered, were living 'on the verge of hunger'.

Between the turn of the century and the outbreak of the
threatened war in 1914, the position of lower-paid wage
earners was greatly improved both by legislation and by
trade union action. New laws provided for unemployment
insurance, a system of labour exchanges and the regulation
of 'sweated' trades. New trade unions like the Amalgamated
Society of Railway Servants recruited all grades of workers.
Old trade unions began to organize on an industrial rather
than a craft basis. Both groups sought and won wage
increases for the lower-paid.

These developments, and others which followed as the century wore on, led the way to great increases in bodily health and in physical maturity. In 1901 the average age at which girls married was 25·6. By 1968, it was 22·7. And if girls were marrying earlier, they were also staying on longer at school, and many more were going on to further or higher education. This process, and the raising of the school-leaving age to sixteen in 1972, have reduced the number of single girls coming into the labour market from the schools, as well as the time they remain on the market before withdrawing to bring up their children.

But other factors are causing an increase in the number of married women seeking to re-enter the labour market once their children are of school age. At the beginning of the century a woman marrying at twenty-five or thereabouts might subsequently expect to bear five children and be a child-minder well into her fifties. By the time she was sixty she might well be dead, unless she was a member of the comfortable classes. Today, that woman's grand-daughter can expect to live until seventy-eight, perhaps fifteen years more than her ancestor. She will have two or three, rather than five, children, and she will have them earlier. In 1969 four out of ten of the year's brides were under twenty-one. Furthermore, contraception has made it possible for women to set an earlier term to pregnancies.

Given that the result of these factors is to shorten the time a girl spends as a single school-leaver and as a married child-minder, then it follows that the period between the time when her youngest child is no longer totally dependent, and the time of her retirement at sixty is correspondingly longer. The expansion of this period means that a married woman is now available for paid work outside the home for a much longer time than ever before.

Our ill-used great-grandmother might have ten years between freedom from the care of her children and death. By contrast, her great-grand-daughter may have all the children she plans to bear and have placed them at school by the time she is thirty-five. In more and more cases that age is likely to be thirty. Between thirty-five and sixty lies a quarter of a century of – what? To increasing numbers of women, the answer is not 'of staying home,' but of going back to work.

Enough, that is, now to account for over half of the female work-force, compared to a tenth before the last war. But still two thirds of the married women in the country do stay at home. Many of these perhaps would like to return to work, and will do so as the children grow older. Others, perhaps having sampled what the labour market has to offer the married women re-entrant, prefer to stay at home, family budget permitting. Indeed, as one looks at the facts, it becomes surprising not that so few but so many married women take paid employment, given the obstacles placed in their path.

We now have a situation in which, for the first time since women's work was taken out of the home by the Industrial Revolution, married women are able and willing in large numbers to rejoin the labour force, without being conscripted by government or driven by economic misfortune. In fact, going out to work is in many ways simply more attractive than staying at home. First there is not enough work to detain a woman full-time in many modern homes, especially once the children are at school. Not only are there fewer children but homes are becoming easier to manage. By the end of the 1970s about two in five households should be living in houses built since 1960. In such houses the old backbreaking and time-consuming chores have no place. And the household jobs which still have to be done are made easier. Washing machines for instance are becoming more common, as are launderettes. In 1970 about two-thirds of all households owned a washing machine.

Other factors help to tilt the balance in favour of going out to work. In Great Britain, for example, the school day usually finishes in mid-afternoon and children may therefore be away from home until 4 p.m. or later. A hot lunch is usually available at school. Most larger places of work have a canteen in which they serve meals which are at least hot, if not particularly appetizing. In West Germany, on the other hand, where the school day can end at 2 p.m., married women have a correspondingly shorter time in which they are available for work outside the home. The availability of meals at school and at work also reduce the amount of cooking and of shopping that is demanded of wives and mothers.

In 1965 the National Plan stated that 'activity rates in the country as a whole are higher now than in 1943, at the height of the mobilization of resources in the Second World War'.[2] In 1943, however, there existed a coherent if occasionally unpopular plan for the employment of women, including married women. Today, no such plan exists. In 1943 women as a matter of urgent national necessity were given or had thrust upon them access to a far wider range of jobs than at any time since the First World War, or indeed since before the Industrial Revolution.

By 1941, the war cabinet was pondering a study by the Ministry of Labour, showing that, because of the expansion of war industries and the diversion into the forces of male workers, there was a labour shortage of 300 000. In 1968 a peacetime government was looking for a minimum of 400 000 more workers to fulfil the growth targets of the day. Within a month of the wartime estimate, there had been conscription into the labour force of women on an age basis, a process that went on throughout the war until even married women of fifty were being put to work.

As we have seen, the National Plan brought out a survey of women's employment, designed to find out 'why women, particularly married women, enter or do not enter the labour market . . .'.[3] It discovered that the reasons why it is thought appropriate that women, and particularly married women, should be confined to low levels of responsibility in disadvantageous types of employment have changed little in a century.

For example, it is widely assumed by employers and, indeed, by many women, that the economic role of a woman is secondary to that of her role as a wife and mother, whether actual or potential. From this follow a set of assumptions that leave little room for the consideration of a woman's individual qualities and aspirations. At one time, women used to stop work on marriage. Today, this is more likely to be with the arrival of the first child. The withdrawal from work was at one time final, since child rearing finished within only a few years of infirmity or death. Such work as was available was either performed at home, or carried on part-time, and it was in any case very poorly paid.

Today it is no longer enough to think of married women as a pool of unskilled, part-time or casual labour. Yet, by and large, this is the case. This is not to say that married women seeking to return to work are discouraged solely by stupid or hostile employers. Married women are for many reasons ill-equipped to take many employment opportunities even if they were offered. There is no doubt that more could be done to help them at this point in their lives. But we should first look at the difficulties faced by such women in the nature of their status as wives and mothers, and then go on to external influences.

Consider the position of a mother who has decided to return to work after an absence of anything from five to fifteen years. What job should she go after, and how? How will she prepare herself for the job, and how can she fit it in among her responsibilities to husband and children? Nancy Seear argues that the professionally qualified woman – a doctor or a nurse – can keep in touch with her profession even while at home either by reading or through people she knows. She may even be able to continue working part-time. She knows where to look for the work, how it can be fitted into her home life and, on the strength of her earlier training, she will be confident of being able to do a good job. She will also be able to see that, although the gap in her professional career may mean that she is unlikely to reach the top, at least her work will be useful, adequately paid and personally rewarding.

If so, says Baroness Seear, she will be unlike many of the many women seeking re-entry into the labour market.

For the great mass of women in every country the position is quite different. They have had no specific training. With a gap of ten to twenty years their knowledge of the labour market, always sketchy, is now both limited and inaccurate. Their views of jobs are highly coloured by the jobs they knew a decade ago. But while they have been at home the labour market and the jobs in it have been continuously changing. Such a woman does not know quite what she wants to do, or whom to ask. She knows she can run her home, even though that does not always pan out; but will she be able to keep to a timetable, to learn new jobs, to compete with youngsters who look like the women's glossies, to be part of a team she does not control. Her husband and her children are doing rather well. She does not want to make a fool of herself, or to take a job they and the neighbours do not think much of. After all, she is a wife and a mother. She is used to running her own show. What's more, she has got to go on running it. Her family does not seem to mind her working – she might prefer it if they seemed to mind a little more – but this may well not last if life for them becomes a little less comfortable, a little more uncertain. She is, as has been said, both under-confident and over-confident at the same time – under-confident in relation to her real capacity for tackling new tasks, over-confident by virtue of her status.[4]

For such women, the Baroness argues, the prime need is vocational guidance. They need to discuss their circumstances with someone able to understand the psychological, practical and vocational aspects of re-entry.

Such a person should be equipped to help build up

self-confidence and a realistic appreciation of what taking a job means. The need for vocational guidance is widely appreciated in the United States and in Sweden, where help is available from the state. In Britain, however, Lady Seear found that help was available only

in the type of work in which women have traditionally been employed and where there are quite exceptional labour market shortages. The new initiatives in the training field which are taking place in the United Kingdom have, so far, had little impact on the position of women, nor is the changing technological and demographic position in the country being reflected in a changed approach to women's jobs.[5]

Thus in 1971 there were occupational guidance units staffed by professionally trained specialists in only twenty-four of the Department of Employment's centres throughout the country. In addition, there were refresher courses available for professional women, specifically doctors, nurses, teachers and social workers. Even here, however, there were problems. Among doctors, for example, there was a shortage of part-time openings, with the result that there were still qualified women who wanted to return to work, but who could not be fitted in.

As things stand, the lack of part-time work, the narrow range of employment in which it is to be found, and the low pay in relation to the necessary outlay on clothes, travel and convenience foods, ensure that two thirds of the women who leave the work-force to have children do not return. Of the remaining third, much of the investment put into their education must be regarded as a write-off. The main priority of a woman with children in looking for work may be to increase the comforts she can give her family, or it may simply be to fill the void left by the emptying of the household. She will not necessarily be looking for the work that best suits her capabilities or experience. Above all, the hours of work must fit in with her domestic responsibilities. That is why we find qualified nurses and teachers working as machinists in garment factories.

In wartime, necessity drives governments first to enlist married women as workers and then to persuade employers to make available part-time work. Since 1945 part-time work has been actively discouraged. For a long time employers were required to pay full social security contributions for workers employed for more than ten hours a week.

So tightly costed is low-added-value work that the cost of full social security payments, which are marginal in full-time, high-added-value work, discourages the employment of part-time workers except in areas of labour shortage. Again, the incidence of part-time work in low-pay industries itself deters women from working. The basic problem of the working mother is that she is made to suffer both the disadvantages of any women in employment and the special handicaps posed by the need to look after children, and there is still a broad body of opinion in the country that says that a woman should be satisfied with marriage, a home and children.

There are two problems here. First, as we have already argued, marriage is no longer the full-time career it once was. There are far more years to be spent in an empty house than formerly, and fewer time-consuming household chores. Secondly, marriage itself, though as popular as ever, is by no means the safe bet it may once have been. Between March 1971 and March 1972 the state spent £70 000 in grants to the Marriage Guidance Council.[6] In the same year, over £4·7 million was spent on legal aid in divorce, excluding the cost of administration.

In 1973 Mr Nicholas Tyndall, the chief officer of the Marriage Guidance Council, said that new divorce legislation had resulted in a jump in the number of divorce petitions to 100 000 a year from 72 000 in 1970. Only 300 of 200 000 divorce cases had been referred to counselling services, despite a provision in the 1971 Divorce Reform Act that solicitors must certify to courts that they have discussed reconciliation with clients and told them of people qualified to help. It must be remembered that a woman who finds herself divorced with a couple of children is at a discount in the remarriage as well as in the re-employment market.

So far, we have concentrated upon the position of the married women who for one reason or another might wish to resume work. An argument that has throughout modern times been used to dispute the admission of married women to the work-force is that they, unlike men, are only in it for pin-money, and that there is already a wage coming in from a husband. Yet there are in this country many single mothers as well as wives who have been divorced, deserted, widowed or otherwise forced to fend for themselves.

In 1973, the National Council for the Unmarried Mother and her Child estimated that there were about 650 000 one-parent families which would include about 1 million children under sixteen. Most of these families revolve around a lone mother. It is not known how many of these mothers do go out to work but, according to the Council, 'many single as well as other unsupported mothers wish to work and be independent of Supplementary Benefit but cannot afford to do so even with Family Income Supplement'.[8] It was estimated in 1970 that even among unsupported mothers working full-time, poverty was so extensive that 54 000 would qualify for Family Income Supplement.

11. Second thoughts set in

The progress of human society consists . . . in . . . the better and better apportioning of wages to work.
                    Thomas Carlyle, *Past and Present*

For improving the condition of women, it should on the contrary, be an object to give them the readiest access to independent industrial employment, instead of closing, either entirely or partially, that which is already open to them.
                    John Stuart Mill, *Principles of Political Economy*

If women workers have missed the boat as far as fair employment is concerned, this is to a large extent because the trade unions wanted it that way. Until a century after the first Trades Union Congress, held in 1868, trade unionists rarely took women workers and their problems seriously; when they did, it was to see female employment as a threat to the interests of male workers. One result of this has been that until well into this century many of the biggest and most powerful unions have either excluded women from membership or from certain employments. Another has been to weaken the organization and bargaining power of women in the industries to which they have secured entry, and to hold down both the level of their earnings, and of their few male co-workers. Not until 1968 did equal pay become a serious political issue, that being the year that a Labour government produced proposals for legislation.

The TUC threw its weight behind the proposals, supporting a tougher Act than actually got on to the Statute Book. Yet eighty-three years had elapsed since the TUC had first formally declared itself in favour both of the principle of equal pay and of helping women's unions to organize in support of the principle. There are today about $2\frac{1}{2}$ million women in trade unions, about 28 per cent of the total female work-force, compared with $8\frac{1}{2}$ million men, just under half the male work-force.

Although there is a long way to go before women become as organized as men, the number of women trade unionists has been increasing faster than that of men throughout the 1960s. In 1972, according to Department of Employment calculations, the number of unionized women increased by 5·4 per cent (147 000) and that of men by a mere 0·7 per cent (60 000). Behind these figures lies the story of the huge increase in the numbers of women entering the work-force, and stagnation in the size of the male work-force. But only about a sixth of the TUC's 150 or so affiliated organizations has more women than men, and there are some unions without any women members at all.

Despite the recent growth in female unionization, membership has long hovered around the 25 per cent mark, or about half of that for men. Thus while the number of women in unions is rising, so is the number not in unions. Workers who are employed in industries where there is a low degree of unionization, as in shops, have their wages and conditions governed by wages councils. Almost without exception, workers fare worse under wages councils than they do under collective bargaining between employer and trade union.

But it is not only at membership level that female participation is weak, albeit growing. In the National Union of Tailors and Garment Workers, for instance, women make up over eight in ten of the membership, but of the forty-four officials all but nine are men. In 1972, the general council of the TUC had two women members out of a total of thirty-nine. The Transport and General Workers' Union, 13·6 per cent of whose members are women, has one woman official and 599 men.

It was in the early 1950s that the trade union movement,

noting the growing ratio of women to men in the work-force, began to ask itself why women seemed reluctant to join unions or to take a more active part in union activities. In 1953 a national survey of women's involvement with trade unions showed that although women were active in the movement, this was usually at local rather than national level, especially in unions where women were in the minority. In fact, there are so few women at the top in the unions that the TUC General Council has to designate two of its seats for women to ensure some measure of direct representation for one-fifth of the Congress's membership.

Historically, of course, the low level of unionization among women derives, first, from the fact that before the general availability of contraception most women saw their stay in the employment market as temporary; and, secondly, from the attitude of many educated women working in shops and offices, who for social reasons refused to join an organization which until the 1960s was thought to be purely working-class. Even today many women who will join a union are nevertheless precluded from playing an active part in the evening's meetings and educational activities because of the need to put housekeeping and domestic duties first.

Many are part-time workers who do not see the connection between union membership and improved conditions. Furthermore, women in shop and clothing industries for the most part work for firms employing a mere handful of people. Here, according to the TUC Women's Advisory Committee, 'there is not only the problem for the union of contacting a multiplicity of establishments, but also of persuading the workers concerned that victimization will not follow trade union membership'.

These are, however, relatively recent preoccupations of the modern trade union movement. For side by side with the narrow and fragmentary nature of women's employment there is a long tradition of unhelpfulness on the part of male trade unionists.

Women's entry into industry and into trade unions developed in a way that was bad for women, bad for industry and bad for trade unions. But the reasons for the unions' new interest in the recruitment of women do not primarily come from concern for women workers as such. More important, perhaps, is the great growth since the last war in the numbers of women at work, up by a fifth in the last twenty years, compared with less than a tenth for men. Also, now that the unions have drifted into stormy waters in the decade since the mid-1960s, they have come to need the membership of women nearly as much as women need them. As the unions have become big, rich and powerful, so have they become convenient Aunt Sallys for inept governments. The Industrial Relations Act, introduced but quickly disowned by the 1970–4 Tory government, threatened to sap union strength by making it easier for one union to poach members from another, and more difficult for unions to attack employers who took on non-union labour.

With the number of women in the workforce increasing at a faster rate than that of the men the unions see in women an obvious and important reservoir of membership, and therefore funds. It may seem ironic that this renewal of interest in women's trade unionism should have been sparked off by the good old bully-boy capitalist dynamic of growth rather than the tenderer notions of solidarity and brother- or sisterhood. But now, as in 1815, trade unions are creatures of industrial society, however poetically their aims may be enunciated. This time, women are being admitted to trade unions on equal terms with men, paying the same dues and, thanks to the Equal Pay Act 1970, receiving a fairer share of union spoils.

We have seen how the abundance and consequent cheapness of female labour tempted employers of the last century to break the convention that a respectable woman was one who was supported by her male relatives. In this regard it was public rather than private employers who first followed this notion through to a mutually satisfactory conclusion, without the stark exploitation and inhumanity of the earlier experiments in the new industrial areas. Nowadays it is in public employment that the first stage, that of seeing and seizing the main chance, has given way to a second and more flexible stage, where steps are taken to get the best out of the people involved.

This is obviously of great importance for the many women who work for the state, whether as employees of local government, or of the Civil Service. It is also important because the example of intelligent deployment of human resources is a valuable stimulant of change elsewhere.

The Civil Service, in contrast to its cautious, tea-drinking image, has for many years been the single most innovative employer of women in the United Kingdom, far more so than supposed bastions of progressive thinking, such as the universities or the schools. The Civil Service found itself an employer of women by accident, and has remained a substantial and comparatively intelligent employer by design.

Large numbers of women began to enter the service as clerks during the First World War, by which time the typewriter was in common use in British offices. By the time of the last war women were able to apply for senior grades of the service, the universities having in the meantime been thrown open to women. However, it was not until 1946 that married women were eligible to apply for posts.

Another rule that went by the board was that women should resign on marriage. This particular regulation seems to have come into being at the turn of the century, as a result of pressure from male clerks, when the Commissioners tried to flood the service with women, hoping thereby to keep down pay rates. By the middle of this century, the employment of women clerks had long been a feature of private as well as of public employment, and the Civil Service found it was no longer enough just to offer employment where others would not. Steps had now to be taken to induce women staff to stay or, at least, having had children, to return.

The first problem which the Civil Service employers had to face was that the large numbers of women employees had had such a downward drag on pay levels that it was becoming difficult to attract men, so that the Civil Service was thrown back even further upon the labour of women. Secondly, the men in the Service had early in the century begun to recognize that only a policy of equal pay, i.e. higher pay for women, would save the ground from being further cut away from under their feet. Thirdly, some women began early to take an interest in union activities.

Their grievance was that although they were admitted to the Civil Service, they were debarred from its higher appointments by the rule that marriage entailed resignation, and precluded re-entry into the Service. After the last war, and the removal of these anachronisms, women still found it difficult to get on unless they were either single or childless. The hindrance was now the difficulty of re-entering the Service at the same level of responsibility as that at which they went out. Thus by 1972 there were more women than men in the Clerical section of the non-industrial service, although they outnumbered men in only two grades, clerical officer and clerical assistant.

These are the two lowest grades and, in the words of the then Head of the Home Civil Service, Sir William Armstrong, 'not regarded by anybody as very good jobs'.[1] If we look at the next grades, executive officer and higher clerical officer, we see that of the 26 000 officers, there were two and half times more men than women. Evidence, one might think, rather of a desire to staff Sir William's 'not very good jobs' than of any advanced ideas regarding a fairer deal for women and a more intelligent use of their abilities. Nevertheless, if women were still denied numerical equality of opportunity, they at least achieved equal pay where they were doing the same jobs.

The decisive factor in the Civil Service was that we convinced the male members of the Civil Service Clerical Association that equal pay was in their interests. We went to meeting after meeting, we faced conference after conference, and we always won the vote on the basis that a man was a fool who allowed himself to be undercut by some little girl filling in time between leaving school and getting married. . . . Furthermore, if men allowed themselves to be steadily undercut they could well find themselves displaced from whole areas of work.[2]

This recognition of shared interests was a factor in the achievement of equal pay in the non-industrial service over a seven-year period between 1955 and 1961, a full decade before equal pay became official government policy. Until 1971 the service had been a pacesetter in isolating and exploiting the potential of female labour. Then that same shrewdness led to a conclusion that from now on the key figure in the market was not the single but the married woman. Much as in 1870, a review was carried out, this time to see, first, how far senior married women might be given part-time work, a concept barely thought about in the professions before then; secondly, how it might be made easier for a woman to combine marriage and a career in the Service; and, thirdly, what re-training might be given to help women return after child-rearing.

In the event, the committee of review went into the subject of women's employment even more fully than that. First among its recommendations was that a woman should not be debarred from any job on the grounds of her sex. The committee further recommended that it should be easier for married women and men to get leave, paid or otherwise, to deal with family emegencies, and that women who did leave to have children should be able to return to similar levels of responsibility.

The curious feature of the review was not the novelty of

its conclusions, but that its deliberations excluded the industrial service, where the need for reform was if anything more pressing. Industrial civil servants are employed mostly by the Ministry of Defence in ordnance factories, dockyards and storage establishments. Among the 200 000 manual workers, there are only 35 000 women. Most of them are confined to 'domestic services', that is, swabbing floors and serving the other civil servants' tea. Not only do the women work in smaller numbers and in a narrower range of employments, but where they do the same work as men they have for many years been denied equal pay. Where it was necessary for women to do 'men's work', it was only on the understanding that they were 'liable to be displaced at any time by men'. This went hand in hand with a series of union agreements under which women were sometimes to be refused promotion to supervisory posts on the grounds that, where men are in a majority, they often refuse to be supervised by a woman. What then accounts for the difference between this male hegemony and the enlightened self-interest of the non-industrial service?

The answer is that the non-industrial civil servants are organized into purely Civil Service unions free to bargain with management as best befits their view of their own interest and that of the Service. On the industrial side, however, the workers are in craft and general unions which represent comparable workers in outside industry. These unions have negotiating machinery separate from that of the non-industrial Civil Service unions, and the same as those which operate in industry at large. In the words of a service memorandum, therefore, 'attitudes in the Industrial Civil Service still tend to be more a reflection of those in outside industry than those in the non-Industrial Civil Service'.

In the case of the latter, it will be remembered, it was the attitude of the unions towards equality that emboldened management to work towards its achievement. In the former, the attitudes of workmates helped to perpetuate inequality in the sight of the very same employers. In any given situation, unfairness is not necessarily the product of employers' attitudes: if anything, it is as likely to be the result of the attitudes of men, be they managers or managed, and of the degree to which women choose to accept the situation.

12. Equality and the law

If you cannot make people good by Act of Parliament you can make it much more difficult for them to be bad.

Lord Soper

We should be very careful not to make something a new wrong that does not strike reasonable men as wrong at all.

Lord Conesford

The late 1970s may one day be seen as the time when British society called a halt to one of the longest-lived and most spectacularly wasteful excesses of the Industrial Revolution, the inequitable treatment of working women. For, as we have seen, from the end of 1975 an Equal Pay Act is scheduled to operate wherever women are doing work that is the same or broadly similar to that being done by men, or, where different, has been rated as of equal worth by a job evaluation scheme.

Secondly, the act was to be backed up by legislation that will make it unlawful to discriminate unfairly on sex grounds between men and women in employment. This would establish the right of women to be considered on individual merit as candidates for jobs normally done by men, and within those employments to equal access to training and promotion. Between them, these two pieces of lawmaking are meant to put an end to a 'tradition', namely that women are by custom or law excluded from some employments and confined to others, while failing to secure equal treatment in pay or prospects in employments which they share with men.

Measures such as these, if exploited by women, would go far towards completing the admission of women to industrial society on something like equal terms with men. It is less than a century since women have been allowed to retain full ownership of earnings and property after marriage, although during the course of a divorce the woman may now claim a share in property even if she did not contribute money of her own when it was bought. As late as 1945 Cambridge University was still refusing to award its degrees to women.

Yet as each of these wrinkles in the fabric of our society has been ironed out, one inequality has persisted and, to a degree even worsened. This has been the treatment of women in paid employment. For the whole of our present century, women have made up a third of the work-force. Twice in, 1914 and in 1939, they proved to be a most capable labour resource when men were called to the ranks from offices, factories and public transport.

In the last twenty years, the number of women in paid employment has increased by one fifth, while that of men has changed hardly at all. Most of that increase as we have seen, has been accounted for by married women returning to work. These now make up two thirds of the female work-force, compared with one tenth before the Second World War. But the treatment of women as workers is in contrast with the growing importance of women as a dynamic component of the labour force, and as our only reserve of labour in any time of national stress. More women do jobs not normally done by men than do the same jobs as men. The women who do the same jobs as men in industry are paid between a half and two thirds of a man's basic rate, a figure that has hardly changed this century.

Woman's work in industry is generally confined to areas like shopwork, catering and food preparation, which combine drudgery with low pay and weak trade union organization. In the professions women can no longer be excluded but they are discouraged from straying far beyond nursing,

F

social work and teaching, none of which is notable for high pay, considering the workload. In addition, women are disadvantaged at every stage of the education that precedes the choice of a job.

It is only half a century ago that girls were given the legal right first to secondary education and then admission to university. But the continuing inequality of the workplace has so coloured the attitudes not only of Ministers of Education, but also of teachers, parents and of the girls themselves, that this opportunity has never been used to the full. The practice of the Industrial Revolution, less than 200 years in the history of these islands, has fashioned a particular role for women: why educate or train them for anything else?

That role has been seen as, first, that of wife and mother and, secondly, as a provider of unskilled, low-paid labour between leaving school and starting a family. So short a working life has therefore never been thought worth either a prolonged education or one able to equip a girl to do anything other than the usual women's jobs. The effects of this outlook are felt at many levels. There is the school that discourages girl pupils from following natural interests in science or mathematics, or encourages school-leavers to aim for colleges of education rather than university. At work, there is the employer who has fixed ideas as to which are men's jobs and which women's, and often male trade unionists of similar views. Girls have less chance than boys of securing apprenticeships, day-release or thorough on-job training. And, to make matters worse, many girls have been conditioned out of even wanting any of these things.

Much of the impetus for change since the last war has come from dissatisfied professional women. They have found that, even though the professions are by law open to women, they are by custom closed, unless a woman agrees to keep to the socially acceptable professions such as nursing, teaching or social work; or, if she will not stick to these, to accept that there is little chance of re-entering her profession at anything much above ground level after leaving to have children. Only if she either does not marry or does not have children will she have anything like the same prospects of advancement and fulfilment as a man. For outside the acceptable professions there are few facilities for refresher courses to ease married women back into their work, while there is a deep and lasting suspicion of the idea that anybody can be a part-time lawyer, doctor or accountant: the idea that a married woman could or should split her time between job and home has yet to catch on.

Dissatisfactions caused by such attitudes, and by antiquated laws that do not permit working women tax relief for home helps, have given rise to much of the agitation for a new look at inequalities between men and women in pay and opportunities. Local authorities, too, are beginning to object to a system that compels them to give university grants to girls as to boys, only to find that, because of antiquated social customs, girls with superior degress may be forced to find jobs as secretaries to boys dimmer than themselves.

Beneath these obvious areas of dissatisfaction, however, it is difficult to conclude other than that, for every woman who complains, there is another content or at least resigned to rubbing along in the groove to which society has assigned her. Were it otherwise, the remedies proposed in equal pay or anti-discrimination legislation might never have been necessary, or if necessary, at least not so long or so often postponed. In this apparent apathy, women are probably little different from men; it is the disadvantaged situation of women that is different.

Legislation extending the vote to women on equal terms with men was not followed by great advances in the standing of women. Pressure from articulate women helped to bring about legislation offering working women similar pay and conditions to men. But this latest round of lawmaking in itself no more guarantees significant advances than did the

former. This is, after all, the third time in the twentieth century
that a period of national stress has been accompanied by a
reassessment of the relationship between the two roles of
woman, as a worker and as a wife or mother. On the previous
two occasions, things have later settled down to 'normal' or
to something like it.

Twice during the course of wars calling for the use of vast
citizen rather than small professional armies, it has become
clear that the country could not function in the absence of so
many men workers so long as women were confined to
'women's work'.

Today, committed as we are this century for the first time
to a standard of living above subsistence level for workers
and their dependants, two things are happening: first, there
is a recurrent inability to meet demands for skilled labour
in times of industrial expansion; and secondly, there is a
developing demand for services based upon unskilled and
semi-skilled labour, as for example in public transport in
the big cities. But these needs can no longer be met from a
male work-force which has hardly increased in twenty years
and is unlikely to increase for a further twenty. It would be
politically difficult to import more immigrants, who in any
case would bring with them a limited range of skills. And not
until there is a radical change in attitudes to women working
will women be able to plug these gaps.

In particular, there must be some new thinking to attract
more married women back to work. This might involve
more spending by government and by employers on courses
to prepare the older married women for re-entry to the
labour market. Secondly, the range of jobs thought unsuitable for women must be greatly revised. There are some signs
that the latter is happening in advance of legislation. London
Transport workers, for instance, have at last (in the face of
a serious staff shortage) withdrawn their opposition to
women drivers on buses and underground trains. The
P & O shipping line now recruits women as radio operators

aboard some of its ships. A widening of job opportunities will help girls while at school to prepare themselves for jobs outside traditional women's work.

Yet how strong is the impetus towards equal pay and a more equitable measure of job opportunities? With the former the difference between today and 1919 and 1944, when the question last received serious discussion, is that an Equal Pay Act is now upon the Statute Book. That in itself, however, is no guarantee that the right to equal pay will be significantly extended. After all, while the United Kingdom did not get an Act until 1970, both France and West Germany have had equality between men and women written into their constitutions since the end of the Second World War. The Netherlands was in 1972 in fact the only member of the European Economic Community in which neither the constitution nor legislation provided for equal pay. Article 119 of the Treaty of Rome, the agreement that binds together the members of the EEC, requires adherence to the principle of 'equal remuneration for the same work as between male and female workers'.

Yet when in 1972 Evelyne Sullerot reported on hourly wages rates throughout industry in the EEC she found that in France women's rates were a fifth lower than those of men, while in the Netherlands and Luxembourg they could be as little as a half. 'In practice, the national legal systems have not given effect to Article 119 of the Rome Treaty which has remained a dead letter as far as the business world is concerned for lack of legal safeguards.'[1] The differential that existed in France after a quarter of a century of legislation was no better than that of the United Kingdom on the eve of equal pay by law. In France, as in Britain, the problem has not been one of lack of law, but of lack of the will to put the law into effect.

There has never been widespread enthusiasm in the United Kingdom for equal pay and equal opportunity. If there had, both would have been achieved long before now.

But that is not to say that the case has not long been argued. 'Resolutions on equal pay were discussed and accepted,' reported a woman member of the Amalgamated Engineering Union after a 1968 conference.[2] 'This subject becomes more difficult each year, if only because it becomes harder each year to find something new to say in support of this principle.'

As we have noted, the Equal Pay Act, passed in 1970, to become law five years later. A male-dominated trade Union Congress declared itself ready to support the claims for equal pay of workers in the women's trade unions in 1885. Even before this, the economist John Stuart Mill had devoted part of his immensely influential book, *The Principles of Political Economy* (1848) to 'consideration why the wages of women are generally lower, and very much lower than those of men'. One reason was custom, grounded either in prejudice or 'the present constitution of society', which 'making almost every woman, socially speaking, an appendage of some man, enables men to take systematically the lion's share of whatever belongs to both'.[3]

We do still have prejudice, although the property and earnings of a woman no longer automatically become her husband's on her marriage. But we still have the other prime cause listed by Mill, that the remuneration of the 'peculiar employments of women' is greatly below that of employment of 'equal skill and equal disagreeableness carried on by men' Mill attributed that differential to the overstocking of female employments, which he blamed on the 'flagrant injustice' not opening industrial occupations freely to both sexes.[4] Mill was over a century ahead of his time. But although his ideas are regularly exhumed and dusted over to this day, an abiding commitment to equality in the workplace has yet to come to pass.

We have sketched in briefly the circumstances surrounding the current interest in making the work-place more attractive to women. A look at how the Equal Pay Act and associated proposals for legislation on sex discrimination came about is this country may prove instructive. Despite examination of the extraordinary role played by women as workers during two world wars, the government of the day had on both occasions set its face resolutely against any acknowledgement of women's role as a permanent feature of the work-force. Members of a Royal Commission reporting on the subject in 1946 said they could agree neither on the reasons why women were paid less than men, nor on the effects of equal pay in industry and commerce.

If it were introduced, the Commission said, then it should be confined to non-industrial government employment where it would cause less trouble. From 1955 onwards, the government began to phase in equal pay for its non-industrial women employees. This did not, however, mark the start of a general commitment. The Commission had pointed out that in most professions women were paid the same as men (although, of course, women have far less chance than men of getting into most professions, and of staying in once they have had some children). Government thus had no option but to bring in equal pay for its own non-industrial employees if the service were to remain competitive.

The two professions employing large numbers of women, nursing and teaching (outside universities) were in effect staffed by government employees and there were different rates for men and women. As we have seen, sex discrimination in teachers' pay had become a political flashpoint towards the end of the war. During the passage of the 1944 Education Act there was a move to abolish the separate, lower pay rate for women teachers. The revolt was quelled only when the Prime Minister, Winston Churchill, made the reimposition of sex discrimination the subject of a vote of confidence.

The stumbling block has always been a mixture of brute prejudice and economic convenience. When in 1969 the Department of Employment costed equal pay in thirteen industries employing many women, the cost varied from an average of 2 per cent of labour costs in engineering, to 13 per cent in shopwork and up to 18 per cent in clothing. From firm to firm the range was from nil to 32 per cent. A 1966 survey by the Ministry of Labour put the cost at between £600 million and £900 million depending on how many of the seven million women not receiving equal pay were subject to equalization.

In 1919 the International Labour Office adopted the principal of 'equal remuneration for work of equal value'. This was subsequently reaffirmed and adopted as Convention 100 in 1951. The United Kingdom was one of the last developed countries to ratify the Convention, becoming the seventy-first state to do so twenty years later. The United Kingdom had never been keen to increase her labour costs by implementing equal pay throughout employment. By 1968, however, the Department of Employment, at the prompting of a Labour government, was circulating the TUC and the CBI for comment on proposals leading to the Equal Pay Act of 1970. That year marked the fiftieth anniversary of female suffrage, and there were calls for action on equal pay in that year's TUC. Neither of these facts, however, was the clincher in the decision of labour to bring forward the proposals or of the Tories to support them.

The real issue was that, once again, Britain was moving towards another attempt to be accepted as a member of the EEC. Among the conditions of entry would be adherence to the principle of 'equal remuneration for the same work as between male and female workers', the narrow definition of equal pay adopted by the EEC in 1958 in article 119 of the Treaty of Rome. British trade unionists wryly noted that the article, dead letter though it was, got into the Treaty not so much through Brussels' concern for women's welfare so much as a political tactic by the intransigent French. While Britain at the end of the last war settled for keeping women teachers' pay a few pegs below that of men, France and the new Federal Republic of West Germany indulged in expiatory exercises concerning something the British did not even have, the constitution.

The French, anxious to commemorate the activities of women in the Resistance, recognized in the preamble to the constitution of 1958 the right of women to equality with men in all fields. France approached the formation of the EEC saddled with equal pay legislation which, although widely evaded, left her potentially uncompetitive in terms of labour costs with other members of the proposed community. In this the French could count on the support of the Germans, who were now anxious to be as conciliatory as possible to their former enemies.

Moreover, in an effort to dissociate the new republic as far as possible from the Third Reich, women were to be assigned a new role. The Nazis had not used German women as wartime labour to anything like the same extent as either the British or the Americans. Their role had been seen as bearers of little party members and as comforters of the decreasingly victorious forces of the Fuehrer. Henceforth, therefore, Article 3 of that country's constitution laid down that German men and women, too, should have equal rights.

British legislation, when it at last came, was stronger than anywhere else within the community, where there were many weaknesses written into national legislation meant to give effect to the supranational Article 119. As the Department of Employment circulated its proposals, the TUC and CBI were quick to line up on opposite sides. The CBI wanted a definition of 'equal pay' similar to that of Article 119, while the TUC were for Convention 100. 'Equal remuneration for men and women workers for work of equal value', the ILO definition, could lead to pay increases for more women workers than if equal pay were given for 'the same work', as advocated under the Treaty of Rome.

As the Royal Commission had observed in 1946, ' "Equal pay for equal work" will not, as used by us, have the same

import as "equal pay for equal value to the employer".[5] In
addition to differences of definition, the trade unions wanted
implementation within two years, and the CBI, if at all,
within seven.

In the event, neither side got what it wanted. Mrs Castle,
then the Secretary of State for Employment decided on a
five-year run-up. The Act itself requires that women employees shall receive equal pay where employed in 'like work' to
men, as will women whose jobs, though different, are given
an equal value to men's by a job evaluation exercise. Mrs
Castle estimated that of the female work-force of about
9 million, over 1 million were already receiving equal pay.
Of the remainder, about 3 million were doing the 'same or
broadly similar' work as men, or would benefit as collective
agreements were altered to eliminate discrimination between
men and women as directed by the new law. Others were in
jobs already covered by job evaluation schemes, while nearly
$2\frac{1}{2}$ million were in jobs where pay and conditions were
determined by wages councils to which the government
was a party.

Altogether, she thought, about 6 million women would be
directly affected by the new legislation. On top of this there
would be others who would benefit from what she called 'the
halo effect'. This, she explained was what happened when
women did not qualify directly for equal, i.e. higher, pay,
but would nevertheless get rises so that the firm could stay
competitive with others in the locality where women were
getting rises through the law.

A curious feature of the passage of the legislation was
the extent to which the Act was criticized by friends of
the government and the Opposition alike. Apart from the
root-and-branch opposition of Tory backwoodsmen typified
by Robert Bell, the MP for Buckinghamshire South, the
main criticism was that the measure did not go far enough.
'Legislation,' said Mrs Castle, 'cannot cover every possible
development, and, in any case, it is no part of my

job to make it unnecessary for women to join a trade union.'[6]

In their study of the Act,[7] Peter Paterson and Michael Armstrong listed six ways of evading the spirit while keeping the letter. Jobs could be re-graded on the basis of the degree to which the work was heavy or light, automatically discriminating against many women, a classic Continental response to Article 119. Jobs performed both by men and women could be cut back so as to avoid direct comparisons.

Jobs currently done by women at women's rates could be graded as jobs open to both men and to women. However, the job descriptions would not match any work presently being done by men. The minimum rate, which would have to apply to both sexes, could be pitched lower than the existing minimum for men, so long as it was not below any nationally negotiated rate. Employers could refuse to introduce job evaluation on the grounds that it would encourage pay claims. Terms and conditions of employment could be varied at different plants within the same firm to discourage comparisons between them. Lastly, an employer could simply refuse to hire women, granted that their labour was now to be more expensive. It could be argued that the increased absenteeism and higher turnover rates attributed to women would make them a less sensible proposition than men paid at the same rates.

The Royal Commission had written in 1946, ' "Equal pay for equal work" is primarily a battle-cry and in a battle-cry it is proper to expect power rather than precision.'[8] To W. K. Wedderburn, a socialist academic, the 1970 Act was a 'quite unnecessarily obscure statute'. For a start it was called the Equal Pay Act, but then went on to talk about rights to 'equal treatment as regards terms and conditions of employment' which seemed to imply that it was about more than pay. If so, then the Act was self-contradictory, for it then went on to specify a list of excluded matters, including pensions, Pensions were both part of pay and of working conditions. They were also an area in which there was outstanding discrimination between men and women to the disadvantage of women.

Professor Wedderburn found himself in strange company in his contention that the Act, either through vagueness or omission, did little to protect the jobs of women whose labour was now more expensive. That is, the Act increased the price of women's labour without widening the range of job opportunities open to them. His views were echoed by Robert Carr, soon to succeed Mrs Castle as Secretary of State for Employment when a few months later the Labour government lost office. He drew attention to the 'silence' of the Bill on the question of equality of opportunity in employment. Although designed to prevent discrimination in the terms and conditions of employment between men and women, the Bill did not establish equal opportunity to apply for jobs or training courses. There was, for example nothing to stop the Stock Exchange or the printing industry from keeping their doors barred to women.

However, Mr Carr was in agreement both with the spirit of the Bill and of the idea, uncongenial to many Conservatives and to many Socialists, that law should intrude into the field of collective bargaining.

My answer to the first question of whether this [equal pay] can and should be assisted by legislation is definitely in the affirmative. It is a legitimate function of the law to put on record the judgement of the community about what is fair and reasonable. It is also a useful and legitimate function of the law in practical terms, because law does form opinion and influence behaviour.[9]

Mr Carr, out of office, was very eager to strengthen the Bill by further legislation on the issue of widening job opportunity. Two years later, however, the Tories, now in office, were taking a very different stand about just such a piece of legislation. This was an Anti-Discrimination Bill, a measure several times brought before the Commons as a private members' Bill as the 1970s began. In essence, the Bill would have made illegal the discrimination between men and women in matters of education and employment on sex grounds alone, and would have established an Anti-Discrimination Board with the power to adjudicate in disputes. Despite Mr Carr's position on the value of law in 'putting on record the judgement of the community about what is fair and reasonable', the Tory view two years later seemed to have changed.

Speaking during one of the unsuccessful attempts to secure a second reading for the Bill, Robert Sharples, an Under-Secretary at the Home Office, said that the government supported the objective of the removal of discrimination against women in every field. But while wanting women to share equally with men in those areas open to both, he added, 'We do not believe that legislation, particularly the Bill now before the House, is the right way of bringing this about.'[10]

In the event, the government came around, alarmed first by the unpopularity of attempts to block the Bill and then by the evidence of discrimination secured by a Select Committee of the Lords, established at the initiative of the Liberal peer, Lady Seear. What it did was to steal the reformers' clothes by bringing forward a Sex Discrimination Bill of its own, covering education and employment. The promise was made during a debate made possible by the offer of Parliamentary time by the Labour Party.

There have been examples before of legislation that seemed to promise much but delivered little, because women have failed to exploit the opportunities open to them. Together with the enfranchisement of women over thirty in 1919, there appeared the Sex Disqualification (Removal) Act. This said that 'a person shall not be disqualified from the exercise of any public function, or from holding any civil or judicial office or post, or from entering or assuming or carrying on any civil profession or vocation, or from ad-

mission to any incorporated society, and a person shall not
be exempted by sex or marriage from the liability to serve
as a juror'.

In 1966 Lord Justice Salmon described the Act as 'a most
important statutory provision which, so far as I know, has
never yet been considered by the courts.'[11] He was hearing
an appeal by a woman who had been refused a licence by
the Jockey Club. While doubting whether horse-training was
a vocation within the meaning of the Act, he allowed the
appeal. The woman, however, did not pursue her case and
so remained frozen out.

We are now at the stage when both of the two biggest
political parties have admitted that legislation should be
enacted to tackle inequalities in women's employment.
However, both equal pay and equal opportunities are
predicated upon a growth economy and full employment,
neither of which is assured in the world in which Britain
finds herself in the mid-1970s. As the decade wears on it
appears that women are once again aware of their unfavourable situation compared with that of men in the labour
market. Whether that awareness, and measures which ac-
company it, are more likely to survive current economic
troubles than those which followed the last two wars belongs
to another story.

Notes to chapters

CHAPTER 1

1. *Women in Britain*, Central Office of Information, 1964.
2. *Hansard*, House of Lords, 14 March 1972.
3. *Report of the Committee on Women in Industry*, Cmnd 167, HMSO, 1919.
4. Office of Manpower Economics, *First Report on the Implementation of the Equal Pay Act*, HMSO, 1972.
5. Hunt, Audrey, *A Survey of Women's Employment*, HMSO, 1968.
6. *Second Special Report from the Select Committee on the Anti-Discrimination Bill* (HL), HMSO, 1973.

CHAPTER 2

1. *Report of the War Cabinet Committee on Women in Industry*, HMSO, 1919.
2. Trevelyan, G. M., *English Social History*, The Reprint Society, 1948.
3. Pinchbeck, Ivy, *Women Workers and the Industrial Revolution 1750–1850*, Cass, 1969.
4. Plummer, Alfred, *The London Weavers' Company 1600–1970*, Routledge and Kegan Paul, 1972.
5. Plummer, op. cit.
6. Pinchbeck, op. cit.

CHAPTER 3

1. Halevy, Elie, *A History of the English People*, Pelican Books, 1937.

2. ibid.

3. ibid.

4. Barber, J. T., *A Tour Throughout South Wales*, quoted by Halevy, op. cit.

5. Gaskell, P., *Manufacturing Population of England,* 1833, quoted by Patrick Rooke, *The Age of Dickens*, Wayland, 1970.

6. *Women in the Trade Union Movement*, TUC, 1955.

7. Gutteridge, Joseph, *Autobiography*, quoted by Valerie Chancellor, *Master and Artisan in Victorian England*, Evelyn, Adams and Mackay, 1969.

8. Hammond, J. L. and Barbara, *Lord Shaftesbury*, Pelican, 1939.

9. Report on Mines, 1842, quoted by Pinchbeck, *Women Workers and the Industrial Revolution, 1750–1850*, Cass, 1969.

10. Hogg, Edith F., 'The Fur-Pullers of South London', from Goodwin, Michael, *The Nineteenth Century*, Pelican, 1951.

11. *Report on Women and Children in Agriculture*, 1843, quoted by Pinchbeck, op. cit.

12. Reiss, Erna, *The rights and Duties of Englishwomen*, Sherratt and Hughes, 1934.

13. Woodham-Smith, Cecil, *Florence Nightingale*, Pelican, 1955.

14. Pinchbeck, Ivy, *Women Workers and the Industrial Revolution 1750–1850*, Cass, 1969.

CHAPTER 4

1. *Women in the Trade Union Movement*, TUC, 1955.

2. ibid.

3. ibid.

4. ibid.

CHAPTER 5

1. Woodham-Smith, Cecil, *Florence Nightingale*, Pelican, 1955.
2. Taylor, A. J. P., *English History 1914–1945*, Oxford University Press, 1965.
3. Barnard, M. C., *A History of English Education from 1760*, University of London Press, 1963.
4. Smith, Sydney, *Works*, Longmans, 1869.
5. Ensor, R. C. K., *England 1870–1914*, Oxford University Press, 1936.
6. Garrett, A. A., *History of the Society of Incorporated Accountants 1885–1957*, Oxford University Press, 1961.

CHAPTER 6

1. Pankhurst, Sylvia, *The Home Front*, Hutchinson, 1932.
2. ibid.
3. Taylor, A. J. P., *English History 1914–1945*, Oxford University Press, 1965.
4. Hancock, W. K. and Gowing M. M., *British War Economy*, HMSO, 1949.
5. Calder, Angus, *The People's War*, Cape, 1969.

CHAPTER 7

1. Seear, Baroness Nancy, in the second reading of the Anti-Discrimination (No. 2) Bill, 1972, *Hansard*, 14 March 1972.
2. Sullerot, Evelyne, *Woman, Society and Change,* Weidenfeld and Nicolson, 1971.
3. Sullerot, Evelyne, *The Employment of Women and the Problems it raises in the Member States of the European Community*, Commission of the European Communities, 1972.
4. Inverview with author.
5. *The Times*, 5 August 1972.

6. *The Work of the Youth Employment Service, 1965–1968*, HMSO, 1968.

7. Evidence to Expenditure Committee, 26 July 1972.

8. Hunt, Audrey, *A Survey of Women's Employment*, HMSO, 1968.

9. ibid.

10. ibid.

11. *Sixth Report from Expenditure Committee*, HMSO, 1973.

12. ibid., p. 130.

13. *Report of the Hairdressing and Allied Services Industry Training Board for the year ended March 31*, HMSO, 1971.

14. Evidence of Mrs M. Cooper, general secretary, Institute of Careers Officers, *Sixth Report of Expenditure Committee*, HMSO, 1973.

15. 'Women at Work: the small child gap and other problems', *Personnel Management*, February 1972.

16. Evidence to the Lords' Select Committee on the Anti-Discrimination Bill, 1972.

CHAPTER 8

1. *The Times,* 2 January 1972.

2. 'The Employment of Women', *Sixth Report from the Expenditure Committee 1971–1972*, House of Commons Paper 182, HMSO, 1973.

3. Select Committee on the Anti-Discrimination (No. 2) Bill (HL), *Minutes of Evidence and Proceedings of the Select Committee. Session 1971–1972*, HMSO, 1972.

4. Seear, Baroness Nancy, *The Position of Women in Industry, Two Studies in Industrial Relations,* HMSO, 1968.

5. Select Committee.

6. 'The Employment of Women', op. cit.

7. Quoted from *Women in the Trade Union Movement*, TUC, 1955.

8. Chesney, Kellow, *The Victorian Underworld*, Pelican, 1973.

9. *Report on the Hours of Employment of Women and Young Persons Employed In Factories*, HMSO, 1969

10. Select Committee.

11. 'The Employment of Women', op. cit.

12. ibid.

CHAPTER 9

1. Select Committee on the Anti-Discrimination Bill (H.L.), HMSO, 1973.

2. ibid.

3. ibid.

4. ibid.

5. *The Accountant*, 2 March 1972.

CHAPTER 10

1. *Maternity Leave*, Income Data Study No. 58, 1973.

2. *The National Plan*, Cmnd 2764, HMSO, 1965.

3. Hunt, Audrey, *A Survey of Women's Employment*, HMSO, 1968.

4. Seear, Baroness Nancy, *Re-entry of Women into the labour market after an interruption in employment*, OECD 1971.

5. ibid.

6. Commons question by Edward Bishop, MP, *Hansard*, 12 March, 1973.

7. The *Guardian*, 21 May 1973.

8. 'The Employment of Women', *Sixth Report of the Expenditure Committee, 1971–1972*, HMSO, 1973.

CHAPTER 11

1. Select Committee, Session 1971–1972, HMSO, 1972.

2. Challis, G., in the *Report of Equal Pay Conference*, TUC, 1968.

CHAPTER 12

1. Sullerot, Evelyne, *The Employment of women and the Problems it raises in the Member States of the European Community*, Commission of the European Communities, 1972.

2. *A.U.E.W. Journal,* July 1968.

3. Mill, John Stuart, *The Principles of Political Economy* Longmans, 1872.

4. ibid.

5. *Royal Commission on Equal Pay 1944–1946*, HMSO 1946.

6. *Hansard,* 9 February 1970.

7. *Equal Pay,* Kogan Page, 1972.

8. *Royal Commission on Equal Pay 1944–1946*, op. cit.

9. *Hansard,* 9 February 1970.

10. *Hansard,* 28 January, 1972.

11. The *Guardian,* 3 January 1974.

Index

Compiled by Gordon Robinson